PRIORITIES

PRIORITIES

Choosing an Ideal Life

by

Jean d'Or Nkezabahizi

A BOOK ABOUT GOD,
PEOPLE, AND FULFILLMENT

iUniverse, Inc.
Bloomington

PRIORITIES
Choosing an Ideal Life

iUniverse books may be ordered through booksellers or by contacting:

iUniverse
1663 Liberty Drive
Bloomington, IN 47403
www.iuniverse.com
1-800-Authors (1-800-288-4677)

ISBN: 978-1-4759-1340-8 (sc)
ISBN: 978-1-4759-1341-5 (hc)
ISBN: 978-1-4759-1342-2 (ebk)

Library of Congress Control Number: 2012906720

Printed in the United States of America

iUniverse rev. date: 04/23/2012

Recognition

I want to take this opportunity to thank my good friend Paul Mason. Thank you, Paul, for your enthusiasm, knowledge and wisdom in the process of working with me to ensure that my book will reach its full potential. The discussion and thought that we have shared has brought us even closer together and has inspired me in many different ways. Thanks for the love and kindness God has placed in your Heart!

What They See
in Jean d'Or Nkezabahizi

Jean d'Or is a young man who has an incredible story to tell of God's protection and grace. It is a story of hope in a life's journey from a Burundian—challenged childhood, to Canada as an immigrant, to a writer and motivational speaker whose hard work and integrity inspires others not to give up but to press forward to accomplish their dreams. Jean d'Or has many goals and aspirations: to be a blessing to the less fortunate and to those who are hurting, and to make a significant difference in their lives.

Elizabeth Schmalz
President of Widows' Strength International

In the years that my wife and I have been welcoming newcomers to Canada we have met many young men but few have become as close as Jean d'Or Nkezabahizi. From our first meeting on the day of his arrival in Canada he has impressed me with his motivation to not just survive but to excel. In the first days of our friendship—when our verbal communication was limited—I knew that this young man was intelligent and wise beyond his years. He had seen and experienced suffering; in fact he was suffering loses, loneliness and culture shock. But, his first thoughts were of his

Mom and the family left behind. As his days in Canada extended into years, it was inspiring to see his strength of purpose grow. Through hard work, perseverance and the grace of God, Jean d'Or is achieving important goals in his life. His story is one that will inspire others to not only seek survival but the best that God has for them!

Jim McNair
Director—Matthew House Refugee Ministry of Fort Erie

Courageous, passionate, and committed are a few words that say much about the character of Jean d'Or Nkezabahizi. His love for, and loyalty to, others, especially his family and friends, was apparent from the first time I met him. So, too, was his love for His Savior. He is a faithful servant of God!

Grass will never grow under Jean d'Or's feet! He is hard-working, creative, and forward-looking. I am impressed with his commitment to what he does. Not content with the status quo, he is ever looking ahead. Yet, he is no idle dreamer. Jean d'Or is a doer! I am sure he would say that I encourage him.

But, as iron sharpens iron, Jean d'Or inspires me. His grace through trying circumstances sets him apart from so many others who have dealt with far fewer challenges. That is but one of many reasons why I am pleased to call him my friend!

Rev. Gary Screaton Page, Ph.D.
Registered Psychotherapist
Chaplain

It's been many years that I have known Jean d'Or and worked together with him in a business that we own. He is: Open-minded, business-oriented, leadership-skilled, and trustworthy. He is everything that you look for in a friend; he has it all. Jean d'Or has a positive attitude that would make many people want to connect with him.

Jude Akom
Business Owner

I first met Jean d'Or while I was serving on the Matthew House Board. With his warm, friendly smile of greeting, he made an immediate impact on my wife Leanne, and me.

At subsequent meetings—possibly a brief encounter within the Matthew House doors or during an annual barbecue to celebrate newcomers, old and new—Jean d'Or was always the same fellow. Our greetings did extend to affectionate hugs of enduring friendship.

When Jean d'Or asked if I would consider proofreading his manuscript for this book, I felt privileged to be of assistance. It allowed me a special opportunity to lend my teaching experience to such a worthwhile endeavour!

Today, I can verbalize what I feel in my heart: 'Jean d'Or is an enthusiastic young man, a positive role–model for young and old, and a true messenger of God!'

Paul Mason
Retired Elementary School Teacher

I'm privileged to be a good friend of Jean d'Or! Since I have known him, he has inspired me in many ways. He has unique talents and courage to do things that most of us may find very hard to accomplish. He is a motivator! God has instilled wisdom in Jean d'Or's heart for the benefit of this new generation.

Albert Tattech
A university Medical Student

PRIORITIES

Choosing an Ideal Life

Contents

Foreword

Today in North America, we are living in an age of great economic uncertainty and instability. Every day in the news we hear dire predictions about a future economic meltdown, possibly even worse than anything we have seen in the past. In this climate of fear and uncertainty, many people are desperately trying to find the secret to a happy and prosperous life. But what they often don't understand is that true happiness and real prosperity can only be found in an abiding relationship with Jesus Christ. He alone is the one who we can trust in as the solid foundation for our lives and the One who will provide for our every spiritual, emotional or material need.

In the book you hold in your hands, my friend Jean d'Or lays out some vital life lessons that will help you to live the abundant life that God has planned for you. Jean speaks out of his own experience in seeing God prove himself faithful over and over again in bringing him through difficult and challenging times both in his native Burundi and in his adopted home here in Canada. My prayer is that as you read this book, you will be challenged afresh to commit your finances, your relationships and your life to "Him who is able to do immeasurable more than all we ask or imagine."

Rev. James McBeth
Pastor, First Baptist Church,
Fort Erie, Ontario, Canada

Dedication

This book is dedicated to all Believers and non-Believers around the world who want to be fully successful and live an Ideal life. It is reaching out especially to those who are struggling with how they relate to both God and treasure (money).

Expectations

PRIORITIES

Choosing an Ideal Life

This is a true story about God, People, and fulfillment. This book provides a simple formula that explains, step by step, how we should live our lives successfully. It is about rich people on earth who aren't experiencing full happiness and how a chance meeting can change a life. The story talks about a man who lived all of his life considering his treasure (money) as his first choice until we had a confrontation at a gas station.

The change in his life starts after I pick up and return an envelope containing $20 000 which had fallen under his car. When we first meet, his behaviour is unacceptable. After several meetings, this man, whose eyes were blinded by his treasures, comes to know the truth and is able to see what really matters in life. Please read the whole story to find out how his life is fully enriched.

Chance Meeting at a Gas Station

About a year after I had graduated from Theological institute, I decided to go back to college to study business. I was nearly two months into my first semester at college and it was almost time for mid-term exams.

Since moving to Hamilton, Ontario, I had been living in a very tiny room in a basement. Due to my allergies, I could not stay there; so, I requested that my landlord move me into a larger room upstairs that was unfurnished. Being new to Hamilton, I did not know where to shop and was not yet able to find my way around easily. Hamilton is a big city, divided by the Niagara Escarpment into upper and lower parts. When travelling up the rock–cut road to the Upper City, it feels like you are entering a different city. But, it is all part of Hamilton and I enjoyed getting around.

I did not have a bed in my small room, and, as my back had been hurting from sleeping only on a comforter on the floor, I decided that I would get a bed after moving to my large room. My landlord advised me to check the IKEA store since they might be having a sale. I took the advice and went to check it out. Since my car had a mechanical breakdown, I asked for a ride from my friend, Emile. He was too busy to drive me to IKEA; but, he allowed me to use his car. As I was on my way to drop him off at school and head to the IKEA store in Burlington, I noticed that the car needed gas. I pulled over at a gas station; as I was pulling up to the pump, I was cut off by a beautiful black Range Rover.

"Sir, you saw me going to use this pump," I told the man who was driving the Range Rover.

"Oh well—sorry buddy," he replied with an arrogant voice.

His actions towards me came as a shock, but I kept my cool. 'I am not going to let him mess up my day,' I thought.

Surprisingly, the man was very well put—together considering his actions; he wore a perfectly fitting and expensive suit, shoes, and tie. Everything about him was classy, certainly not the look of most people who act unprofessionally. I figured that he may be late for a business meeting.

"Maybe he is a drug dealer or something. Look at the car he drives," my friend Emile said.

"Well, he could have asked to use the pump first . . . of course I would have let him," I said aloud.

After the man finished pumping gas into his car, he opened his driver side door; an envelope dropped to the ground, but he didn't see it.

I got out of the car, picked up the envelope and waved to get him to stop; but, he paid no attention.

Looking into the envelope, I was shocked to find that it was filled with cash. "Sir, you dropped something!" I shouted and waved my hand in the air for him to see me. He saw my hand waving, but he ignored it and kept on going.

"Let's keep it man! Who knows where he got this money . . . he was rude anyway?" Emile said.

"No! That's wrong and it's a sin to take someone's belongings," I responded.

"Come on man! He has been acting evil," Emile added.

"It's ok. That's the reason we should not keep it. We are Christians and we believe in God. Do you remember what Jesus answered to the Pharisees' disciples and Herodians who questioned him about paying taxes? I think it's written in Matthew 22:15-21."

"I can't remember. What did he say?" Emile questioned.

"Jesus answered: 'Give to Caesar what is Caesar's, and to God what is God's.' You mentioned yourself that it could be drug money. If that's the case, let's give it back to whom it belongs because it does not belong to us at all and is not even a blessing from God. Let's keep our hearts pure for our God. And besides, we saw who dropped it. Please! Let's not argue about this; I am giving it back to him," I said loudly.

Two ladies were standing near some other pumps; they had seen all of this man's bad behaviour towards me.

"Why do you have to bother anyway? He wasn't nice to you," one lady said.

"Do you know him? What's in the envelope?" the other lady asked.

"It's money, lots of money," I replied.

"Wait! We can keep it! Can I see it?" the first lady asked.

"No, I have to get it back to him," I replied. 'What's going on with people nowadays?' I thought.

"Are sure you want to do that?" the first lady asked.

"Yes, I am positive. I am a Christian and I cannot take what doesn't belong to me," I replied.

Since the man refused to stop, I did not have time to pump gas into the car. I followed him and tried to give him the sign to stop; but, he was going quite fast in a 50km zone. I didn't know what to do other than to just keep following him. As he approached a traffic light and stopped, I was able to get closer to him. I kept flashing my headlights on and off but he didn't want to stop. In my mind there were so many different voices telling me to keep the money, take the money to the Police station, or to keep following him until he stopped. I ignored the negative voices and kept following him. As he approached an on-ramp to the 403 Hwy towards London, I realized that I would not have enough gas to follow him. I decided that, if he refused to completely stop, I would have to take the money to a police station. Finally the man pulled over just before the on–ramp. He stepped quickly out of his vehicle with an angry expression, as though he was going to punch me.

"What do you want from me, boy?" He demanded.

I held out his envelope and told him that it had fallen at the gas station when he opened his car door to get in.

As he accepted the envelope, his face suddenly went pale. In a subdued manner, he said, "I am very sorry; I don't know what to tell you." His voice was filled with regret and shame was displayed on his face.

"You should apologize to us and give us at least something," Emile's voice came from inside the car.

"No, it's ok. It happens," I replied.

"I was coming out of a business meeting and going to another one when we met at the gas station. I was already late; I did not think that you would let me use the pump first. Believe me, I have had a really bad morning already," he explained.

"Sir, it's all right," I replied.

He took the envelope, opened it, and checked to see that everything was still in place.

"Do you know how much you just saved me?" he asked.

"No sir, I did not count."

As the conversation continued, he extended his hand in introduction.

"My name is James," he said.

"Nice meeting you James; my name is Jean d'Or."

"What a serendipitous meeting," James proclaimed.

We both laughed.

"I've never seen anyone in my whole life—especially a young male—who would pick up a large sum of money from a rude and angry man and still gives it all back. Who are you? What do you do, Jean d'Or?" James questioned.

"Basically I'm a student," I answered. "I just enrolled in college to study business."

"What made you do this?" James asked as he held up the envelope.

"James, I am Christian. I live my life for God; whatever I do should reflect the Image of God."

"I like that God of yours. He must be a good God," James said with wonder in his voice.

"So, what about you James? What do you do?" I asked.

"Well, I'm a businessman. I own business companies across Canada and overseas."

Now it was my turn to be awestruck. I just smiled and wondered what kind of good life James was living. I concluded that he must live in a wealthy neighbourhood—maybe on Toronto Island.

"Where do you live, James?" I asked.

"Toronto Island. Why?"

"Wow, I guessed that one exactly!" I exclaimed with a grin.

There was a short silence as I pondered the man who stood in front of me. This fellow, who owned several businesses across Canada and internationally, lived a high–end life that many people only dream about. He was obviously very educated; yet, during that first meeting at the gas station, he had acted so crudely. I tried to think of a reason for this. 'He must have lots going on in his mind; maybe he needs some of God's love in it,' I thought.

We stood quietly next to each other for a few moments; but, we both had other places that we had to be. So, I extended my hand to say goodbye.

"Excuse me James . . . but I have to go," I said.

"Yes, me too," James replied.

As I turned to go, I heard his voice once again. "Excuse me Jean d'Or. You seem to be a very good young man and you have strong faith in your God. Truly, I know nothing about God. One time I opened a Bible and saw these quotes say things such as: 'follow me, blessed are the poor, be humble, it's hard a rich man to enter the kingdom of heaven, don't care about things of this world.' It just didn't make sense to me. Why do you have to be poor to be a Christian?" James asked.

"God does not ask you to be poor financially but to be poor and humble in your heart. He does not care about your money—just your heart."

"Well, believe it or not, this is my last year in this type of business. I have been in this business for 20 years; but, I feel dissatisfied despite all that I have achieved. My parents introduced me to their business and I carried on after they retired. But I feel that it wasn't my choice."

"Any reason you would like to give it up?" I asked.

"Well, don't get me wrong, I love what I do. I just feel a little unfulfilled. I have made a lot of money, and, I have done much for myself, my family, and my friends. But now I want to take a few years off and think about what I want to do next."

James explained that, although he was very wealthy, he still felt that he lacked a meaningful existence. Despite all his money, he was not truly happy. He had given a lot of thought about what he wanted to do next with his money that would include happiness; but, he was not able to figure it out.

"I am struggling with the fact that my life isn't complete. I have heard about Christianity and God's will, and all that, but I don't know how I can combine my life together with the Christian faith."

James didn't know my concern on this matter. But, now he knew two things about me. He knew that I was a Christian and that I was studying business. Therefore, he thought that I would probably understand what he meant.

"Truly, it is not so difficult to combine Christianity and business," I said.

"Are you really a Christian or are you just saying it to make your point?" James asked.

"Of course I am a Christian since I was a child; I grew up in a Christian home. My father was a pastor and my mother was a singer in the church choir. After the genocide happened in my country, God delivered me and provided for my escape. That changed my life and increased my Christian faith. From that time, I have depended on Him alone."

"Unbelievable! What genocide? Are you from Rwanda?" James asked.

"No—from Burundi which is near Rwanda. We had genocide similar to what happened in Rwanda; but it just didn't get as much news coverage. Basically, it's African troubles. Believe me, I have seen all and it has made a real difference in the way that I see things. I understand what you may be going through," I said.

James pulled out his wallet and tried to give me a reward for returning his money. But, I did not take it.

"No, James—may God bless you for your kindness. Just thank God that I was there when you dropped your money."

We both laughed.

"Please, allow me," James insisted.

"Thank you, but no, James," I replied.

We stood there for another awkward moment and I finally asked, "What exactly are you thinking about in terms of a relationship with God?"

"Well, I think about whether it would be possible for me to be rich and successful as I am today, and to serve God at the same time. How can I serve God without losing all I have worked for?"

"So do you think you cannot be who you want to be or do all things you wish to do and still believe in God?" I asked.

"I don't know, I guess so . . ."

We were about to leave and James reached into his pocket for a personal business card. As he was going back to his car, he handed the card to me and asked me to call him later in the evening.

"Please call me; it was a very nice meeting."

"I will. The honour is all mine," I replied.

After he drove away, I stood there staring and thought, 'What kind of rich man, rides in Range Rover vehicle, lives in Toronto Island, has all the money you can dream of having but is still not satisfied? Oh well, It shows that '*money isn't everything. It is needed to get things done, but it can't fulfil human desires unless God blesses it.*'

When I could no longer see his vehicle, I got in the car.

"Man, I can't believe you found his money and you couldn't even take the gift! How stupid of you. I could really use that money," he exclaimed. "I was already starting to make plans for a little vacation—now, you've just ruined everything," Emile complained.

"I bet you did!" I laughed. "Emile, listen! It's a few thousand dollars; besides, it's someone else's money. Honestly Emile . . . I would rather be wealthy in God than be rich here on earth," I said.

"What do you mean by that?" Emile asked.

"You go to church, you should figure it out. It means that I prefer to be broke and have no money but keep my God's peace. In other words, instead of committing a sin by keeping someone's money, I prefer to keep my peace with God because he is wealthy in His way. I will let God provide my blessings."

"Whatever, buddy. You always push back a blessing when it comes in your way; that's why you will never be rich. Just get me to class," Emile said with a disappointed voice.

I drove to the school, dropped Emile off and continued on to IKEA for my shopping. As I was driving, I thought about Emile and those two ladies who were so disappointed that I didn't accept their wrong advice to keep the money. Then I concluded, *'Being nice changes people's hearts.'*

Calling for a Change

It was about 8:00 p.m. in the evening. I had finished my supper and, while I picked up my phone, I thought about it for a moment. 'Should I call him now, wait or should I just forget about it?' After a few minutes, I decided to call him up to fulfil his request. Also, I kind of wanted to get to know him and learn about his business. I knew that he would have good ideas from his business perspective and I was interested in what he had to say. He seemed to be a successful man; but, he needed some more happiness in his life. That also intrigued me. I picked up his personal business card and dialled the number. After three rings the phone was picked up. It was James.

"James—this is Jean d'Or. We met at the gas station today."

"Yes, d'Or. I am so glad that you called."

"I didn't expect to get to you directly. I figured your maid might answer first."

"No, we don't have an employed maid regularly . . . only on scheduled days when we require help around the house. Actually, I was expecting your call—that's why I was close to the phone. I do that for special people like you, d'Or. You know what? Now that you decided to call, let's meet and pick up where we left off," James said.

"I would love to," I agreed.

"I am looking at my calendar for the rest of the week and I see that tomorrow could be open for breakfast. Can you make it?"

"Sure I can James. I am available for breakfast every time you are available. I am very pleased and look forward to it. I have asked my pastor friend some of the same questions about the Christian life and money. I am sure I can help you to understand and get the answers you are looking for," I said.

"It sounds great to me. D'Or. How about 9:00 a.m. tomorrow? I can pick you up myself."

"Great! I will be waiting in the lobby. Thank you so much, James," I said and gave him my address.

"My pleasure, d'Or! I also look forward to it. Oh! And I hope you don't mind but my wife would like to join us."

"That would be great," I said.

I waited a few seconds for him to hang up as I played with my cell phone in my hand. I paced around in my apartment, full of happiness that I was going to meet up with James—one of the richest men in Canada—to talk about the Christian life. I had a terrific feeling in my heart and I prayed with a quiet voice, "Thank you God for giving me this opportunity to give you glory. Please give me the right words to say when I speak to this man about you."

After the call, I thought of the words which can best express this kind of meeting; I came up with the conclusion that *'you don't wait for opportunities to happen; you have to make them.'* At this point, I needed to pray and to ask for more guidance with how to speak to James. I was also so proud of myself that I did not take the small gift he had offered me. Maybe by taking it, I could have lost the important opportunity of bringing him to God.

Now that I had the opportunity to meet with James, I had to decide the next step. So I decided to call my friend, Frank, to inform him about the exciting news.

"Hello my friend Jean d'Or. How are you?" Frank greeted me over the phone.

"Hello Frank. I am very fine thank you—and you?"

"Fine too, thanks. So what's up?" Frank asked.

"I have some very exciting news to share with you."

"Ok, I can't wait to hear all about it," Frank replied.

So I told Frank the story about what happened and how I now had the opportunity to witness God to James.

"Wonderful, Jean d'Or! I am very proud of you and happy to hear that God is working in you. So what you have to do now is to pray to make sure God's voice of power is within you when you guys meet again. By the way—when are you meeting again?"

"We are meeting at 9:00 a.m. tomorrow; his wife wants to join us too."

"So what do you plan to talk about?"

"I was thinking, maybe, about how our actions reflect the Image of God. What do you think about that?"

"Great," he answered. "That sounds like just what he needs."

"Thanks. I think so . . . somebody needs to turn his attention to God."

We shared a laugh.

"Please let me know how your meeting goes tomorrow with your new friends and let me know if they need to keep up the meetings. Maybe we can include them in our group meetings. That way, you have a backup. You know how we do it," Frank added.

"Yes sir. Definitely! I will try to see if we can meet up again and bring them for the next step. You know better than I. Plus, if they see other rich Christians, it may trigger their minds to follow God too."

"Possibly! Remember to pray."

As we ended our phone conversation, I was too tired to do anything else. I took a shower and headed to bed. Of course, I prayed.

Reflecting God's Glory

The good feelings and excitement I had wouldn't let me fall asleep all night. I tried to rest . . . but I kept tossing and turning. I couldn't wait for morning to come. From time to time, I tend to be late for my appointments; but, for this one, I could not afford to take the chance of being even one minute late! At precisely 8:55 a.m., I was standing outside waiting for them. I looked in both directions; then, I saw a beautiful Porsche Cayenne approach and pull over. The window rolled down and I saw James and his wife.

"Good morning, Jean d'Or. I'd like to introduce my wife, Janette. She came to join us for breakfast."

"Hi, Janette," I said as I extended my hand through the open window.

She shook it. "Hello Jean d'Or. My husband has told me about your kindness. What a nice young man you are! James told me about your faith in God; I couldn't wait to meet you."

"Thank you. Glory is to God," I replied.

As I got in the car, I noticed how nicely they were both dressed.

"You both look fabulous!"

"Oh, thank you; you look great, too," Janette replied.

"Well, we good–looking people are going to have breakfast at the Sheraton Hotel Restaurant in downtown, Hamilton," James said.

"I would love to!" I exclaimed.

"Let's go then!"

While we were going down the hillside toward downtown, I looked around the car I was riding in. It was a very smooth–riding car and it was the ultimate in beauty.

"I love this car! I have heard people talk about the Porsche Cayenne, but I have never had the chance to ride in one. And I didn't know it was this beautiful and comfortable," I complimented.

"Thanks D'Or—it's Janette's car," James said.

We made our way downtown and pulled into the valet parking at the Sheraton Hotel. As we got out, the valet welcomed us warmly. "Good to see you again, James and Janette."

"Yes, Joseph. But, I'm not here to chit–chat with you," James replied abruptly.

"That young valet was being nice to us; there was no need to be rude to him," Janette told James softly.

"He's only working for my tips. If it wasn't for that, do you think he'd be that nice?" James responded.

"That's not true! Not everyone is rude like you," she exclaimed.

They continued arguing about the young valet as we walked inside the restaurant. Once inside, we were promptly seated by the host.

"Wow, is this ever elegant!" I said.

"I know. There are a few nice restaurants in downtown; but, I always love to come here whenever I am in town for my business. I thought it would be nice if we came to this one with you," James said.

We looked over the breakfast menu and made our choices known to our server. While waiting to be served, I opened the conversation.

"Janette and James . . . do you mind if we talk about how one can both have faith in God and be a successful business person?"

"Of course not. Go ahead and bring it on," James encouraged me.

"Great! Well, after we left each other yesterday, I thought about what you had said regarding your business struggles . . . how it is difficult for you to understand the Christian life and how you wonder how those two things—business and the Christian faith—can go together. I remember a time when I struggled with the same issues until I realized a very important concept that I would like to discuss with you. I just couldn't see how I could be successful in business and still serve God; but, one day I met a man who has since become a trusted friend of mine. In fact, you will probably meet him in the future . . . if you still want to continue to learn how you can include faith in God within your business."

"Do I know this man?" James asked.

"I don't know—maybe or maybe not. He is wealthy and also a Christian. His name is Frank McLeod—he really opened my mind," I replied.

"So how did you meet this man?" James asked.

"I met him at a Bible Seminar in 2006 before I graduated from theological studies. He was a guest speaker . . . I had a chance to speak to him afterwards. I told him about my struggles in my faith, work and other things. So, he gave me a special invitation to speak with him in his office so that he could help me to understand my concerns."

The waiter came over to our table and politely asked if we needed anything—coffee, tea or water—while we were waiting for our meal to be served. We all took coffee. The waiter filled our cups and left.

"You look too young to have those kinds of struggles. Anyway, what were your issues and how did Frank help you?" James asked.

"Well . . . I struggled with how my personal character can reflect God's character in everything I pursue. I pondered how I could set up the right goals to inspire others in the right way, keep my promises to God and people, follow God's leading, make sure my self-development goes with God's will and, most importantly, how to handle money and still be godly," I replied.

I paused for a moment and James urged me to continue.

"So Frank said to me, 'Listen . . . every person on the earth who thinks about the Christian life has the same struggles. I myself had the same struggles. Thirty years ago, I was just making a living; but, deep down in my heart, I knew there was something else better than I was doing. The problem was that I couldn't get over the insight I had in my mind about Christianity. I felt like I needed to sacrifice myself or do something drastic in order to become a Christian and maintain my life.' Frank told me that he was getting tired of the life he was living which did not involve God and had no meaning. He revealed to me how he dealt with those struggles."

I continued with my dialogue. "Frank decided to create a networking with people who had a different perception of life—not just occupying their business, but also having faith in God. He sought out people who had done great things with their lives and careers while still being devoted to their Christian faith. He discovered that their foundation of what they had accomplished was based on God's blessing."

"God's blessing . . . hmmm," James mused.

"Yes," I answered. "When I heard Frank's story, it totally changed my mind about how I look at life. Basically, we reflect the image of God—as the Bible defines it; we are created in the image of God and whatever we do reflects that image. Truly, we were made to live for Him so that, in everything we do, we represent His image. That simple truth has changed my thoughts about Christianity in the marketplace," I explained.

The waiter returned with our food and he poured more coffee for us. There were a few moments of silence as we were being served. Then I asked if I could give thanks to the Lord for the food and fellowship we were about to share. The breakfast was so delicious—everything was very nicely prepared. After we finished eating, Janette asked me to continue with what I was saying. I looked into their eyes; they were both curious to hear more about the content of Frank's teachings.

As James and Janette listened attentively, I repeated what Frank had told me. "Usually, in all I plan or do, I ask myself whether or not it will reflect His image on earth. How will people judge my actions? If my heart doesn't feel right about the things that I am about to engage in—about the words I am going to say, or about the plans and goals that I have set up—then it isn't right to do it. It means that God does not support the thoughts or plans I have in mind. The best way to understand this is to follow the concept."

"What concept was Frank talking about?" James asked.

"He was talking about the concept of reading the word of God and learning what God wants for your life. The key to all that is to be more in tune with God's will for your life and allow God's transformation," I replied.

"How do you do that?" James continued to question.

"Frank taught me that God's spirit will lead you. He told me that many people define the Bible differently . . . Some get scared of the Bible because they know that they are leading lives that are not pleasing to God . . . Some comfort themselves with their favourite verses found in the Bible because they think it supports what they are doing . . . Others don't even want to hear about God and His words because they think God is against their success. He continued to tell me that there are many warnings against some ambitions, riches, money and power; but, we should know that all of this is God's creation which He has granted to us to enjoy. The important thing is to make certain that our actions give Him glory and represent His image, rather than misrepresent that image and cause others to avoid God," I recounted.

"What did Frank mean by misrepresentation of that image?" James asked.

"Great question James! Frank used wealth as an example. He told me that there is nothing wrong with being wealthy. Wealthy people who are transformed by God can perform great things with their money on earth. They understand God's love and take the opportunity to be generous because they know everything they have achieved came from God with the purpose of blessing others. But those wealthy people who have not yet been transformed by God miss out on a lot of opportunities," I explained.

"Hm . . . I see," James pondered.

"What Frank meant is that wealth can be used for God's glory; but, it can also be wrongly used. When God gives the wealth, it's a blessing; it has the power to transform people's lives. But wealth without God's blessing leaves people unfulfilled," I added.

"I have never thought or looked at it that way before. I always heard people say that money could create evil thoughts or was the root of all evil; but, I could never figure out why it is the root of all evil. After all, everyone needs it to enjoy life and to be happy," James countered.

I responded. "It is the love of money which can become the root of all evil—not money itself."

"We have money—but, we are not happy or enjoy our life," Janette interrupted.

"Janette . . . let's not get into that now!" James retorted.

"No . . . really . . . did you forget about your behaviour towards me and everyone else?" Janette argued.

The argument continued; so, I decided to try and change the topic. "I would like to suggest several books for you to read. I personally found them to be a great encouragement."

"We'd love to! What kind of books?" Janette asked.

"You could start with this one called 'Become a Better You' by Joel Osteen, published by Free Press in 2007. It is one of my favourite books ever written where he detailed seven keys to improve your life."

"Thank you Jean d'Or . . . we look forward to reading it. Right James?" Janette commented.

"Why not," James added.

As I looked at them, Janette smiled; I felt that a first step had been taken on a spiritual journey.

It was starting to get late and I had to get to my morning class; so, I needed to conclude our meeting.

"Excuse me, Janette and James. My next class is coming up soon and I would like to go get ready for it. Is there any way that we can continue our conversation another time?"

"Of course . . . we would love to. We can't wait!" Janette replied.

"Great! I have spoken to my friend Frank and told him about you. He is in the real estate business, is a very strong Christian, and would be delighted to meet you. Would it be okay if I introduced him to you? He has some very good lessons, which he uses when he leads his Bible study group, that he would like us to learn. Also—if you'd like to come out to the group sometime—there are a few other successful and high–profile people like yourselves. They are part of the weekly Bible study group who, I'm certain, would love to meet you as well. We all come from different backgrounds and have a diversity of ideas and struggles; but, we help each other to understand and learn the lessons we struggle with. It's all about understanding treasure and how that can reflect the image of God on earth. Is there any day or time you prefer to meet Frank?" I asked.

"We would love to come and learn what you have learned. Monday, Thursday or Friday would work for us. So you say that those people are very successful and high–profile; then, who are you really? You're just a student, aren't you? And do I know any of them?" James asked.

"Yes, James . . . I'm just a student." I paused to look at him before I continued. "And, I will arrange a meeting with Frank for Friday at 2:00 p.m. That's the time I am free too. And most of the people in the group are older . . . a few of them are even retired. Frank introduced me to the group a while back. Some of them attended the same Theological Institute as I did . . . These are the people who helped me to understand how business goes together with Christianity. This is especially important, now that I am studying business," I replied.

"Jean d'Or . . . I'm speaking for both James and I when I say that you are more to us than 'just' a student!" Janette spoke determinedly. "By the way—what type of business are you taking in college?" Janette asked.

"I have already graduated from Business studies back in Burundi—Africa. But I decided to go back to College here to strengthen my qualifications. I am in an administration and insurance program," I replied.

"Good for you! So, what is Frank's next lesson about?" Janette asked.

"That I can't tell you. I don't know exactly what Frank is going to teach us; but, I can tell you that it will be a very valuable lesson. I know him and I trust him. However, you already learned that it is important for us to control our actions and behaviours and to ask ourselves whether or not they reflect the Image of God as the Bible defines it."

"Let us drop you off at the college, so you won't be late for your class, and we will meet again on Friday at 2 p.m.," James said in subdued manner. He was still feeling the impact of Janette's words.

James called the waiter for the bill which he then paid. We left the restaurant together. The car was already waiting for us at the front door. He tipped the valet and then we drove off. They dropped me off at the college. I was so happy that I was able to meet them together. The fact that they agreed to continue to the next step was a sign to me that their lives were changing. After class, I called Frank to confirm our meeting for Friday at 2 p.m. I told him the exciting news about what had happened in the meeting with the couple. He expressed his happiness to hear the news, and he was excited for the meeting ahead with James and Janette.

'*It doesn't hurt to have a pure heart towards others,*' I concluded.

Personal Character

It was Friday at 1:55 p.m. I was standing outside my building—waiting for James and Janette—hoping that they would come as they had promised. They were a little late; but, they finally arrived. I gave James Frank's address.

"Oh, I know the way; I have a friend in that area. Steve lives there. You know our friend Steve, right Janette?"

He took Frank's address and put it in the GPS for direction.

"I didn't know Frank lived in the Mississauga area. I thought he may live in the Niagara area because you told me that your hometown is there," James said.

"I am very excited to hear what he is going to talk about," Janette said.

"Me too! I am always excited just to meet him and hear what he has to say. As I mentioned before, we have a group meeting every week. Every other week is for Bible Study and the following week is for activities such as working out or volunteering in the community. Frank always amazes us with his personal character. And the most amazing thing is that, although he is a very busy man, he always finds time for God," I said.

As we drove along the QEW towards Mississauga, we talked about our lives and got to know each other better. James and Janette told me how they met, and how James got into the business that was left to him by his parents who were now retired and living in Italy.

We finally arrived at Frank's home. The property was protected by a big iron gate—his home was large and had a well–manicured lawn.

"Beautiful!" Janette said in hushed voice as they began to have a clear view of the house.

We pulled into the driveway and parked close to the entrance.

"Frank is expecting us," I said.

As we approached, the main double doors opened automatically and Frank was there to welcome us.

"Come in, come in! Great to see you again, Jean d'Or. Who do we have here today?" Frank asked.

I hugged him . . . "It's great to see you too, Frank. Here are my friends I have told you about . . . James and Janette."

Frank extended his hand and greeted both of them.

"I am very pleased to meet you. Welcome to my home . . . I am very excited to get to know you," Frank said with a warm, welcoming voice.

"It's our pleasure to meet you Frank. We've heard great things about you and we couldn't afford to wait another day. You have a beautiful home! My wife and I can't wait to learn from you. Jean d'Or told us just a little bit about you and your teachings and I am certain we are going to learn some valuable lessons." James expressed.

"Well, we are going to have a great time together," Frank said as we followed him through his living-room to the meeting room.

"Please make yourselves at home . . . my chef is ready to prepare drinks for us."

After Frank had taken our orders and left, we had a few moments to talk privately.

"He seems to be a very nice guy! What else does he do besides working in the real estate business you have told us about?" Janette inquired.

"He has travelled around the world doing motivational speeches about personal character and other topics. He is very trusting to God too which makes his character extra–ordinary. He has written several books—my favourite one is about personal growth. I'm certain you are really going to enjoy his lesson today."

After a short time, Frank returned with his chef carrying drinks and four tuna salad sandwiches. "I hope we're all going to enjoy my chef's preparations," he said.

"They look delicious!" I continued. "Frank . . . Janette and James would like to know more about God—how He works in the life of rich folks and I guess how to be wealthy and blessed by God instead of rich without blessing. On our first meeting, we talked about how our actions reflect the Image of God."

"Yes, God works within every open heart," Frank commented.

"Jean d'Or is very good at explaining it . . . but he said you're an expert," James said.

"Well, I'm certainly flattered," Frank said. "But it has been a journey for me as well. Where would you like to start?"

"I'd like to tell you a bit about our situation," Janette offered. "My husband has a problem. Since his parents retired and moved back to Italy, his business has consumed him. It has come to the point that we are slowly losing each other. He cannot control himself anymore . . . he angers so easily! That's actually how he met Jean d'Or. He was very rude to him; but, Jean d'Or kept God's grace in his heart that day. I don't want to go into details because I wasn't there when it happened. My husband told me the story. Maybe if you can touch on that . . ." Janette said.

"Thank you Janette. I am very pleased that you are open to that. I think today we should talk about personal character. I feel that we need to know first how we can develop the right character before we move on to the next step," Frank said.

We all smiled and looked at each other. I could feel a growing sense of comfort within the room.

"In order to develop this right character," Frank said, "you must first learn about God, get to know Him, and keep Him first in your lives. In other words, keep God as your number one priority. If you can proclaim that God is first in your life, you are on the right track. The Bible says in the book of Deuteronomy 13:4: 'You shall follow The Lord your God and fear Him; and you shall keep His commandments, listen to His voice, serve Him, and cling to Him.' When you keep God first in your life, you have nothing else that controls it except for Him. Not even your business or money will control you. Actually, the word 'priorities' is one of my favourite words. Having God in my life as my number one priority makes me feel safe and complete. Many people have different priorities; but, we, as Christians, must prioritize God as number one in our lives. If you succeed in doing this, then your life will be more fulfilling and have greater purpose."

"I get that. But if you are a very busy man, this can be difficult. If God really does know everything, he also knows that I am busy. Why does God give us a life that is so hectic and still expects more from us?" James asked.

"The Bible calls us children of God," Frank responded patiently. "That means we belong to Him and we should not bring any excuse to Him. As you just said, He is the one who gives us life; but, he is also the one who takes it away. So, we need to make certain that we live our lives for His glory. As business people . . . yes . . . we can be busy; but, we know that it is God who is in control."

"Ok. I think I'm getting it. What about you Janette—how do you feel?" James asked his wife.

"I'm still listening and I'd like to hear a little more," Janette responded thoughtfully.

"Great! Now I can see that we are getting somewhere. One of the mistakes we make is that we tend to commit all of our time to other things—like business—and don't leave time for God. But, when God isn't first in our lives, everything we gain we think is gain from our own effort. Money tends to control us because there is nothing else influencing our lives . . . except for money and business. It's like we are blind! We cannot see what's good and bad . . . we cannot feel or hear God's soft voice in our hearts because we are not led by God's spirit in us. We don't even understand how money—or rather its control over us—can be harmful because we think it is everything."

"Yes, that is true. My husband thinks that way and I think it is the reason things aren't going so well at the moment," Janette spoke sincerely.

"Come on, Janette . . . you always blame me for everything that goes wrong. We're in this together—It's not just me. Now that we are getting to know the solution, let's learn it together."

I almost said something to James . . . but, I remained silent.

"I am so glad that we're getting on the right track . . . shall I continue?" Frank asked.

"Please . . ." James urged in a more subdued manner.

"I was saying that, when God isn't involved in our actions or success, we will most likely spiral out of control because 'things' will gain control over us. Some people try to serve both money and God; but, the Bible tells us that 'No man can serve two masters.' You cannot serve God and something else. We all know that money is the most powerful object here on earth. In other words, money plays a big role in our lives. However, you can still serve God and be wealthy at the same time. There is nothing wrong with that. The idea is that you have to know God, learn about Him, and keep Him first. If you do that, then your money and things will not get in your path . . . you will be able to develop a strong personal character and also be able to enjoy your life fully because God is within it."

"What about the verse in the Bible which says that we have to be poor in order to follow God? D'Or has touched on that . . . but I'd like to hear your explanation."

I could sense the seriousness of James' request.

"No, no James. You don't need to be poor in order to follow God. We are not saying that money is bad. But the way that you pursue money makes a big difference. If money is the most important thing in your life, then you lose the image of what the true prize is—a good connection with God. The problem is that, when we replace God with money, we do not reflect the right image of Him. There is nothing more important to God than for us to be conformed to His character or image. And . . . when we talk about His character, we talk about all those qualities that have been created and found in God: love, patience, faithfulness, kindness and other qualities. We, as God's creatures, are supposed to live our lives demonstrating all those wonderful characteristics that represent God's character.

By doing so, we present a positive example of a successful life in the world. People may have the freedom to choose . . . to follow or not."

As I sat there watching the expressions on the faces of the couple, I could feel the presence of God through Frank's message and how the good news was touching them . . . I could feel that James' heart was already accepting much of what was being taught.

Janette was truly a sincere and down-to-earth lady. She attended church . . . but, as yet, she had not fully committed her life to God.

"I have been praying for this," she spoke.

"What do you mean Janette?" Frank asked.

"I mean that I have yearned to see my husband sit down and learn or talk about God. He always said that only those who have nothing to do or those who have lots of problems go to church. He said that it was just something for people who need emotional help or something to feel better about themselves. It's really a miracle to see this happening!"

James interjected. "Look . . . when I was young, I used to go with my parents to church. There didn't seem to be a single Sunday when the Pastor didn't talk about money, problems or things needed for the church. Today . . . Pastors on TV often talk about problems and money. So I have reason not to trust Pastors' preaching."

"All my life," he continued. "I have never had a real friend—especially a successful one—who would go to church to pray. All my friends would go there, only because they needed something. To me, they were hypocritical."

After he paused for a moment, he continued. "But . . . now that I'm thinking about what you're telling us Frank . . . I can see that it's possible to be both successful and live the Christian life. I hadn't thought it was doable until now. I can also see that I have not been interpreting the Bible correctly. Really, it's starting to make more sense to me . . . and I am willing to learn more. Thanks Jean d'Or for bringing us here together," James concluded.

"No, don't thank me. Let us both thank God who made our meeting possible," I said.

It was Frank who spoke next.

"You know James . . . we both had the same wrong perception about God before we learned the truth about Him. We all have different ways in which we learn about God. Some of us learn about Him from true friends and others learn from meetings like the one you had with Jean d'Or. I myself learned from a friend of mine who you are going to meet in the future . . . if you wish to continue with our meetings. She is a very devout woman," Frank said.

"Sorry Frank," I interrupted. "I just want to add this to your lesson. James . . . you mentioned about TV preachers. Some preachers on TV kind of confuse people . . . especially people who are not true Christians or who don't know much about God. The only way to know about God is to read his word—the Bible. Many of today's Christians don't read the Bible; so, they just believe what others are saying or what preachers preach because they have not read the truth for themselves. The key is to read the Book regularly. You will find every human thought in the Bible and you will learn right and wrong from its message. All of God's character and personal qualities are found there. Really, nothing is new that isn't detailed in The Book. All those other Christian books are just there to support what has been revealed in the Bible," I said.

"I would assume you both read the Bible sometimes?" Frank asked the couple.

"Not these days. I used to read it; but, now when I begin to read, it's like it knows that I don't want to spend the time. And . . .

if I read verses such as: don't follow money, no rich man can enter the Kingdom . . . I feel like closing it," James confessed.

Frank and I shared the smile before he refocused on James.

"I suggest that you should start reading it, keep reading it, and don't get discouraged. And also select other Christian readings too, if you can. Jean d'Or told me that he had referred you both to a book to read. Have you started it? It supports what we are learning and what we usually talk about in our meetings."

Frank continued. "Let's move our lesson forward as we discuss personal character. You know, James and Janette . . . people who are not Christians or don't believe in God can't really differentiate between sins and human error or mistakes."

"What do you mean by that?" James asked.

"When non-Christians sin, they don't call it sinning . . . they call it a mistake or an error. They don't know how to tell the difference between human errors and sins. They also don't want to call it a sin because they don't want to feel guilty about something. They are afraid to be judged by their wrong actions. They try to comfort themselves by calling sin human errors. Please let me explain . . . there are mistakes we make that affect our relationship with God and there are mistakes that most likely affect ourselves or our relations with others. Take bad eating habits for example; this mistake only affects us; but, it does not necessarily affect our relationship with God. However, we should keep our body in good shape as it is the temple of God. Do you understand?" Frank asked.

"Hmm . . . yes we do. But, how does sin relate to personal character?" James asked.

"Good question," Frank replied. "Let me try to explain. Do you mind if I use the example of when you and Jean d'Or met at the gas station?"

"Of course not," James replied.

"Thanks . . . James . . . think about the moment when Jean d'Or was pulling over to the same gas pump that you wanted to use. You probably saw him . . . but, you still took his spot anyway. Somehow, you didn't think that it was a sin to ignore others and act rudely toward them. You affected everyone there by your actions. You did not take the time to apologize; but rather, you just took off. The sin that you committed was connected with your personal character. People who were there and saw what happened probably judged your behaviour as rude."

"That's true," James confirmed.

"On the other hand . . . they all probably regarded Jean d'Or as truly a gentleman. So you see . . . by sinning or not having a good personal character affects our relationships both with God and those around us," Frank explained.

"Now it makes perfect sense. Thank you," James responded.

"When we have a good personal character, we will know if an act is a sin . . . even before it is committed. Right, Frank?" I asked.

"That's true, Jean d'Or. We as Christians know when something is a sin. So, when we sin, it is usually done knowingly. But non-Christians don't recognize sins most of the time because they think that they are human errors or mistakes," Frank said. "But mistakes are committed accidentally. The good news is that it's easier to clean away sins than it is to correct our mistakes to gain back our personal character."

"I don't quite understand. Can you explain?" Janette asked.

"I'd love to. When we sin against God, the only way to erase our sin is to repent and ask Him for forgiveness. It only takes few seconds to ask for God's forgiveness; but, when we make mistakes, the consequences of those actions may last a lifetime."

Janette and James considered his explanation; I could sense their seriousness.

"There are times when sin and mistakes have consequences that can make life a living hell," Frank said.

"When, Frank?" James asked.

"I'll tell you. When a preacher, pastor or priest deceives people by teaching a false doctrine, he has committed a sin against God. Even if he is forgiven, he may never be trusted by society again. Many people may lose faith in God because of deliberate sin."

"What a good explanation! That makes a lot of sense to me," James said.

Frank continued. "Everything we do has to give glory to God. We are called to work with Him and for Him within us. As business people, we are to let God be in control of all areas of our lives and business. On the other hand, we are also called to demonstrate our self-control and self-discipline. We have to examine what we do and make certain that it reflects God's character. We must act as disciples of Jesus."

"Hmm . . . What does that mean?" James asked.

I noticed that James was listening intently to what was being said and that he was truly looking for a change in his life. Frank noticed this as well and continued patiently with his lesson.

"Disciples in the Bible were Jesus' followers. They followed Jesus' teaching so that they would be able to carry on his work. That's exactly who we are as Christians—disciples! We do the same. We follow his teaching and, when we do that, we demonstrate God's character on earth. Does it make sense to you now?" Frank asked.

"Yes. What I get from it is that, to be a disciple, you have to apply self-discipline," Janette said.

"Right, Janette. So, did you enjoy today's lesson?" Frank asked.

"Of course, Frank. We just learned how to develop a good character which includes putting God first, knowing the difference between sin and human error, and having self-control and self-discipline. Seriously, we really learned lots today! Wouldn't you agree Janette?" James said.

"Yes . . . Thank you for your message, Frank . . . and thank you, Jean d'Or, for bringing us together today!" Janette added.

"So, you mentioned that you and your group meet once in a while?" James asked.

"Yes, James. We usually meet every week," Frank answered. "In fact, we are having a meeting tomorrow. You are welcome to join us. You will be able to meet others who are more successful in business and they have all kept God first in their lives. Pastor Mark is one of our group members. He was a successful businessman earlier in life; he is now a pastor and he is going to be the main speaker for tomorrow's lesson. I believe that he is going to talk about wealth, right Jean d'Or?" Frank asked.

"I think so," I replied.

"Janette and I would be honoured to attend these meetings," James said.

"Please join us. The meeting is at 4:00 p.m. and we usually have supper together afterwards. Sometimes, we have it here at my house or wherever else the meeting is held. At other times, we eat out at a restaurant. But, tomorrow, we are going to have it here. Don't worry—there will be lots of variety on the menu for everyone to choose from," Frank replied.

"We are positive that we are going to enjoy everything! I can see that your God has really blessed you and works through you," James commented.

Frank smiled. "I can see that somebody already recognizes the power of my God and I am also positive that He is going to be your God too."

"I am getting convinced . . . but . . . I still need to hear more about what I am getting into," James said.

In prayer, we thanked God for giving us the opportunity to learn and to be able to understand the teaching of Frank. James and Janette had an appointment to keep so Frank offered to drive me back home.

"We have to leave; but, thank you so much for everything. Jean d'Or—we can pick you up tomorrow," Janette offered.

"Thank you, but I think that I will drive myself here so you don't have to bother taking me back again. My car isn't in good shape; but it's still running," I replied.

We said goodbye and they left. I stayed at Frank's house and had supper with him.

"Those will be wonderful people to bring to God! He must be happy in heaven," I exclaimed.

"Of that you can be certain, Jean d'Or! And they seem to be quick learners too! I think we should touch on other topics that relate to business and explain how they also relate to God. Since you are taking a business course, Jean d'Or, try to touch on issues such as diversity. Explain how God created us with different talents to fulfil his purposes on earth as one body."

"Yes, I agreed."

We finished our supper and he drove me home.

My day was over and I was very happy with how it was spent. I did what I usually do at night before bedtime. I read my Bible and some other books, prayed, and drifted to sleep. However, the happiness that I had in my heart that night would not let me sleep well. I kept thinking about the couple's change, and how '*one chance meeting can become the opportunity of a lifetime.*'

God's Wealth

I woke up the next day feeling healthy and rich with happiness in my heart for another beautiful day God had provided. I thanked Him for the day that I was about to enjoy. Then, I prepared myself to be ready for a special meeting that we were going to have that afternoon.

When it was time for our meeting, I drove to Frank's house, arriving five minutes early. James and Janette were there already.

"Hello everyone," I said, extending my hand to greet each person in turn. "Hi Frank and Valerie, James and Janette, Mark and Cheng, William and Marian."

Only Thomas had not yet arrived. Out of the entire group, only Thomas and I were single and not running our own businesses. However, he was a professor at the college which I attended.

"Hi, Jean d'Or. God is very pleased with you for bringing our guests to Him. We are very proud of you too," Mark said.

"Let me introduce you to them! This is James and his wife Janette. We can save the story about how we met until after supper," I said.

"Too late! We already know. James told us how you met . . . It's incredible how God works to save people!" William jumped in.

"Yes, it is indeed," I replied with a thankful heart.

Frank brought out a variety of cold drinks including juice, water and iced tea. I poured some iced tea for myself while we were waiting for Thomas to arrive. We were just about to start without him, when he arrived—late, but apologetic. "Excuse me everyone; I had a little trouble at work. Well . . . who have we got here? Some new members?" Thomas asked as he greeted the couple.

"It's great to meet you Thomas! I am James and this is my wife Janette."

Frank stepped forward as our host. "Welcome Thomas. What would you like to drink? There is iced tea, water, and . . ."

"Thanks Frank; iced tea is fine," Thomas politely interrupted.

I could see in everyone's faces how very happy and excited they were to meet the new couple. 'How much happiness there must be in heaven right now for these two people,' I thought.

Frank stepped forward again as our host.

"Excuse me folks . . . but I believe that Pastor Mark is ready to begin our lesson for today. Please, allow me to introduce you, Mark, to these newest guests who don't know you. Pastor Mark was a businessman . . . we started business together. He seemed to be dissatisfied with what he was doing and wanted something else to engage in that would bring him more happiness; but, he couldn't figure out what that 'something' was. To make a long story short, he became a Christian and went back to college for Bible studies.

Actually, he went to the same school some of us attended later in the USA. He is now a pastor. We love him as a true brother and trust him. Right folks?"

"Thanks, Frank, for the introduction. So, James and Janette—Frank has told me a bit of what you have touched on so far. You already talked about reflecting the Image of God and Frank talked to you about developing personal character. So, today I was thinking of talking about God's wealth. The lesson is about our treasure here on earth."

Pastor Mark continued to speak with confidence. "The Bible says that 'Money is the root of all evil.' The passage is often misunderstood; it actually means that money becomes evil if we devote our hearts to it."

"That's true," Cheng agreed.

Pastor Mark continued. "Money is just a piece of paper with a number on it to get our attention. It's an object we use to get things done here on earth. It can be good or bad depending on how you look at it and how much you feel the need of it. We all need money to survive . . . to get what we need; but, when money becomes an obsession—when it takes the place of more important thing in our hearts—that's when the love of money becomes a root of all evil to us. The Bible says in the book of Luke 6:45: 'The good man out of the good treasure of his heart brings forth what is good; and the evil man out of the evil treasure of his heart brings forth what is evil: for his mouth speaks from that which fills his heart.'"

Mark paused . . . then, he posed a challenge to us. "The true question is—what do you love, money or God? Do you want to fixate your heart on the treasures of the earth or the treasures of heaven? When we talk about the love of money, we tend to point fingers at rich people. Yes . . . money can bring pride, self-righteousness, and power to those who have it . . . unless they love God and understand that all the power, righteousness and glory belong to

Him. I think we should all look into our hearts and find where we stand because *our hearts are the foundation of the truth.*"

As Pastor Mark continued, I could see that he had our complete attention.

"The Bible tells us that! 'We are made in the Image of God.' As Christians, we all should know that God is wealthy. All the wealth on earth and in Heaven belongs to Him. If we have faith in God and do what the Bible recommends, He will add blessing to our lives according to His will. *Money which is blessed by God is bonus; it is to be used in a good way to do great things on earth.*"

Mark continued to explain. "Often, we buy a lot of things that we don't need because we have so much money. But folks . . . we can never satisfy our wants unless we have God's peace in our hearts. The Bible says that: 'We should not store up for ourselves treasures on earth; rather, we need to store up treasures in heaven.' I know this is a hard concept to deal with, especially when we have so much and we live in a part of the world where there is everything we seemingly need in life,"

"So what should we do, Pastor Mark? It's not our fault that we have so much; God himself created it. I would call these blessings!" James exclaimed.

"Good point, James. And, I am glad that you just mentioned the word 'blessings.' It's not our fault that we have everything here compared to third world countries. Here in North America, we are more blessed than others. If we look in the Bible, men of faith in God were men of wealth. Canadians—even of average or below average income—are still some of the wealthiest people in the world in comparison with other places. The question is—what are we doing with the wealth that God has blessed us with?"

Pastor Mark followed his question with a strong statement. "Christians or non–Christians should look into their hearts to find out whether they are reflecting a good image. Are they storing up earthly treasure or heavenly treasure? We have to judge our own hearts. We are not to judge others, because we do not know their hearts and we don't know what they have or what they plan to do with their wealth. We see so many rich folks who possess so much—million-dollar bank accounts, million-dollar homes, private jets, the most expensive cars in the world. A question we should ask ourselves is why there are so many poor people on earth while there are rich people who can share their wealth and still have more than enough to live with. Many of the richest people on earth are blinded by their earthly treasures; they don't understand the difference between wealth that is blessed by God and wealth that is not. They will never see the truth of what it means to be wealthy on earth unless they have the light of God in their hearts. As Christians, we need to know that we are blessed to bless others."

Pastor Mark continued with emotion. "If I may . . . I will use my wife and myself as an illustration. A few years ago, we sold our three million dollar private jet. We donated the money to hospitals and orphanages in Africa and built several schools to give children an education. We both felt that there were so many people around the world who need help . . . we agreed that God blessed us with plenty so that we could bless others."

As Mark paused, he continued to speak with a humble heart. "Sometimes, we take too much pride in ourselves and the things we have accomplished. We look at all the hard work that we have put into something and say: 'This is mine and I will spend it the way I want.' But, we forget that it was God who blessed us with the energy and knowledge to achieve all that so that we can then use it for His purpose."

"So, you are saying that we should give up or sell our things we don't need in order to please God?" Janette asked.

Mark shook his head vigorously. "No, no! My point is that we should not point fingers at others who are wealthy. Rather, we should look into our own hearts. We need to look at what God wants us to do with the wealth with which He has blessed us. Imagine supporting two or three young children or new immigrants who become valuable members in community, and then decide to stay in the community which has supported them to achieve their goals. They will bring pride to the community that has supported them; they will most likely help others to achieve their goals too, because they can remember the process that they went through. So, think about how much glory will go to God just for helping some children and how happy you would be just to see the whole community thank God for your support."

"It makes sense," Frank said.

"Truly, I don't even consider the money my wife and I have as our own money. I used to think that way until we became Christians and realized that God owns everything and He is the one who gives and takes away. So my biggest challenge is to decide what God wants me to do with it at any given moment. I pray about anything I am engaged in, whether it's big or small. After prayer, I follow God's lead."

"So how do you know that it's God's lead?" James asked.

"Good question. Before I create a plan, I pray about it. When God approves my plan, He will answer me in different ways. Most of the time, I feel peace and comfort in my heart to go ahead with the plan. For example, I may get a call to donate to a children's charity; if I pray and I don't feel comfortable doing it, it means God doesn't approve of it."

"Ok, I am confused here. Why wouldn't God approve of you helping children?" Janette asked.

"The charity may be fraudulent; or, perhaps God has another plan in mind. Believe me, if you pray to God for something, He will answer. Also, if the answer is yes, I cannot resist but I must go ahead and do what God wants me to do with His wealth. God gives us His capital to use for His purposes. The difference is that we don't pay Him back directly—but indirectly—by doing His work.

I can tell you that *every wonderful gift comes with responsibilities.* Children are an example of such a wonderful gift. They do bring us happiness; but, they come with obligations. Money is the same . . . God gives us money with the responsibility to do good things with the wealth while we are enjoying it."

"Interesting . . . I think I understand now," James exclaimed.

"Please excuse me; I have to check on my chef and ask him to bring us the menu for this evening's dinner," Frank stated.

"This time of fellowship which we can share during dinner will provide a needed break . . . I feel that I have said much already," Pastor Mark exclaimed.

The chef came out with several menus in his hand and a friendly smile on his face. He greeted everyone and handed the menus to us. "Please feel free to choose from the menu or you can make up your own dish. I will make certain that I meet your requirements."

"Nice" Thomas said.

While we were waiting for supper to be served, we shared appetizers that had been brought out for us.

"I think we should have our supper outside on my terrace. It's a very nice evening to enjoy the outdoors," Frank proposed.

We all agreed. We went through Frank's elegant living room and out onto the beautifully decorated terrace with high–quality outdoor furniture. About an hour later, the supper was ready to be served. The chef served each of us according to our orders.

"This looks delicious! We should have all our meetings at Frank's house," Janette spoke with a twinkle in her eye.

After the chef had served us all, he stepped to the side with the words: 'Please enjoy!'

"Pastor Mark . . . do you mind blessing the food? You are the only pastor here," Frank said with a smile on his face.

"Not at all; but everyone here can do it as long as you speak from your hearts," Mark replied, smiling back.

After Pastor Mark said grace, we ate. The meal was incredible!

During the supper, Thomas looked at me and asked, "Jean d'Or—how is school going? It's funny how God works isn't it? I think about how we all met through one person. Look at us now sitting together, sharing supper and talking about God. Praise His name!"

"School is going so well; thank you for asking," I answered.

"I know you are taking business, and you have taken theology. So . . . what do you want to do in your life really?" Thomas asked.

"I think I will use both. My father was both a pastor and an economist. He was using his knowledge in finance to make a living from rich non–Christians and giving free help or support to poor Christians while showing them how to manage what little finances they had. He was very successful at this. I think the knowledge God has given me in Bible studies is to bring more people to Him; the other knowledge involving finance is to help people to understand how money and Christianity work together. I feel that I must especially teach those Christians who think that God will provide everything as long as they remain Christians, regardless of their commitment to good works for God. Don't get me wrong. Yes, God provides; but, not for lazy people! We have to plan; God does not plan for us. God approves our plans as long as they are part of His will."

"So Jean d'Or—how do you know that God approves of your plan? I heard people say that they are following 'God's plan' and you say that God does not plan for us. How can you explain that?" Valerie asked.

"Well, this is what I think. Yes we all say 'God's plan'. Therefore, we try to blame God if our plans don't come through. However, we are the ones who make them and God approves. How do we know that God is in agreement? We can learn it by looking at things such as signs, the leading of the Holy Spirit, and miracles. For example, when a child requests a thing from his or her father, that child really doesn't need to pray for signs or miracles because the father is there physically. Either he will accept or reject the request. And the child can always go back physically to the father for a reminder. The difference is that, as Christians, we deal with an unseen God. It means that when we make plans as Christians, we should pray for answers and wait until God responds. The answer can come as a sign we have requested; it could be a feeling—which is really the leading of the Holy Spirit—or it could even come in the form of a miracle."

I continued with my response. "Going back to your question—this is how we make mistakes. God will never choose for us; God works within our plans. If our plans don't fall into His will, then, they aren't approved. God wants us to be successful and He desires the best for us; but, the choice is ours. Basically, we should plan according to God's Will. *'We have to take the journey to get to our destination.'* The good news is that God's will is for us to succeed."

"It's amazing how something so little can affect so much!" Valerie commented with a smile.

"Yes, indeed. Since I have known Jean d'Or, I have learned lots of wisdom from him. God has blessed his heart. He is a wise young man," Frank agreed with Valerie.

"Yes, I agree. He is. I can't wait for his turn to speak!" Janette added with heartfelt emotion.

While we were waiting for dessert, Frank's chef came and cleared the table.

"I think we should stay here and finish our lesson for today; it's a wonderful evening," Frank commented.

Frank's chef returned with a variety of desserts. As we enjoyed the delectable food, we took a few minutes to just enjoy the weather and each other's company before Pastor Mark resumed.

"Back to the lesson about God's wealth—we left off talking about how we should be using the wealth that God has given us. Folks . . . we are just stewards; this means that we should do what God wants with the money He has given us. We should keep our hands open to any opportunity God provides. I, myself, consider every request as an opportunity to show people God's mercy. Truly, I don't own the money . . . And, It is God who shows how to use it. That's why I call it God's wealth because all we have is His. So, we should learn how to live a lifestyle which includes God," Mark explained.

Then he continued. "As Christians we have a different view of wealth; that's why most people aren't comfortable talking about money and how to us it. But, I feel that we need to learn about it—especially those high profile Christians who are living lavishly. We have to stop judging each other and start encouraging one another with how to do the best we can for God's glory."

"I think we are getting to know more about what God wants from us," James commented.

Pastor Mark's thoughts became very personal. "It's my decision to praise God and serve Him with all He has given me. There are quite a few verses in the Bible that have been helpful to me. 1 Samuel 12:24 says: 'Only fear the LORD, and serve Him in truth with all your heart: for consider how great things he hath done for you.' Truly, look at me today. I am healthy and I can have anything I wish for. Is it really too much to praise and serve God for all that? Look at your own lives; I am sure you will find something to praise Him for. Most of the time, when our lives improve, we don't go back and try to learn where those blessings came from. We too often think that we worked hard to get it; but, we forget that He is the one who actually made those blessings possible for us. But guess what? When we try to deny the truth, we lie to ourselves. That's why we can never feel wealthy enough in our hearts, despite all we achieve. There is passage in the Bible in Ecclesiastes that says: 'Whoever loves money never has enough.' Basically, if you devote yourself to money, you can never get enough of it. You always want more and you will do anything to get it. This takes away your happiness for having money. It takes you away from true wealth because you can never experience the wonderful feeling of giving."

"That is very true. I never thought of that before," James exclaimed.

Mark looked directly at James as he spoke. "If you go out there and ask people who are very rich about how much money is enough for them, many would say that you can never have enough. I am not only talking about rich people either. I am saying that we were all created with different gifts. Even those who seemingly have nothing would be asked to give generously to someone else in need of what they possess. The whole point is to be wealthy in your heart. What does your heart dwell on—money or possessions? Our grandparents lived in a world of 'what's mine is yours—they shared.' We now live in the world of 'what's mine is mine'. It's because we have messed up God's original plan about wealth. Nowadays, people want to keep everything for themselves."

Pastor Mark became personal again. "Therefore, I have figured out that I have to make myself available to be used by God. I take the increase that he has given me and make certain that I keep my heart devoted to him. He keeps my heart clean about the amount of money I have. It doesn't matter how much or little I have—I still have to fulfil His work."

I felt the urge to speak. "I think we should then put it this way: 'We *make money; money doesn't make us*.' In other words, we should be able to control our money and not let money control us."

"Hm, I've never heard that expression. I like it. True . . . we make money; money doesn't make us. We should think that way," Mark said.

"It really sounds true," James said.

"Oh well, its street talk; you folks don't go on the street, so you can't hear every expression," I said.

"I am on the street; I spend more than eight hours with my students. What are you trying to say . . . that we don't know what's going on in the street?" Thomas asked.

"This is what I mean, Thomas. Those students are polite in front of you . . . they can't talk freely about what they are thinking. Most of the time, 'kids teach kids, youth teach youth, adults teach adults.' They are open to me more than they can be open to you; that's when I get the opportunity to teach them about God's love," I responded calmly.

James then spoke. "From now and on, I am going to consider my money as though it belongs to God. Thank you, Jean d'Or, for giving me the opportunity to know you. I am not as young as you; but you did so well. Keep it up! I couldn't have even come close to this knowledge and wisdom. I had always thought that it was me who worked hard to get what I have. But I now know that it is God who actually is the one who works hard within me. I guess my wife and I should truly start serving Him."

"Let us give thanks to God who caused you and I to meet. God works in ways that no man can understand," I responded.

By 8:00 p.m., we were ready to wrap up the meeting for another week and head home.

"I just want to summarize our lesson for today," Pastor Mark said in closing. "We just learned how God's wealth works. It includes:

1. being a good steward of His resources,
2. supporting generously those in need,
3. keeping your heart open for Him, and
4. using God's Wealth responsibly."

"I am so happy that I have met everyone here and that we are on the same page. As the Bible recommends us to stay and pray together, we should do it. James and Janette . . . please stay connected with Christians so you can grow your faith in God," Mark recommended.

"Yes . . . James and I feel the connection already. Thank you all for having us," Janette replied as she looked affectionately at her husband.

"By the way—do you have a church to attend?" Frank asked.

"Not really; but we know of a few. Maybe we should join one of yours. Do you have any recommendations?" Janette asked.

"I know one of the churches in the Toronto area . . . I can take you over," I said.

"Is it the same church you go to?" Janette asked.

"No, not the one in Toronto. However, all churches are good as long as they preach and teach the good news of God . . . and they accept Jesus as our saviour and the one way to heaven," I commented.

"So, what are your plans for tomorrow or next week? I can come and take you over there and show you where the church is. If you like, we can even talk to the pastor . . . I know and respect him," I said.

"Tomorrow sounds good. What time?" Janette asked.

"The morning service starts at 10:00 a.m.; so, we can meet up around 9:30 a.m. in downtown Toronto and go from there," I said.

So we set down the time and place when we should meet. Just then, James' cell phone rang. Although I could only hear his half of the conversation, I gathered that it was his son calling.

"Sorry, but I have to leave. My son needs me; Frank, thank you so much for having us over; we are very thankful. D'Or, let's talk about this tonight over the phone. I will call you later before 10:00 p.m.," James added.

I didn't know just how much trouble James and Janette's son was in . . . I found out later that he had been arrested. Frank and I walked the couple out to their car and watched them drive away. We went back to the rest of the group and prayed before everyone left.

"What's on for next Saturday?" Valerie asked.

"I think we should do hiking at my place; what do you think?" Thomas said.

Thomas—although he was not earning a huge salary through his work—had inherited a large estate from his parents. He owned a number of large and beautiful properties outside of Mississauga.

"I think it's Valerie's turn to teach next. Just for curiosity, what are you going to teach about Val?" Cheng asked.

"Hm, I don't know yet—maybe about salvation. Since James and Janette are new, they need to hear it and accept Jesus as their Saviour," Valerie replied.

"Good point . . . I agree with that," I said. "I can recall that my father used to tell me: 'A good way to preach to rich people is to give them compliments for their hard work and talk about how many good things they can accomplish in God's Kingdom.' Salvation from God is the last thing they want to hear about because they are afraid of feeling judged."

We said our goodbyes to one another and left at the same time.

Love and Forgiveness

I hoped that everything was okay. It was past 10:00 p.m. and James and Janette had not called as I expected. I thought of calling them, but thought better of it due to the lateness.

Just before 10:30 p.m., the phone rang. It was Janette.

"Hello Jean. I'm sorry for the late call, but my husband is still dealing with this situation with our son."

"Hello Janette. I'm sorry to hear about what happened. I was starting to get worried when I didn't hear from you earlier. But how is your son doing? Is he okay?" I asked.

"I am just going to let my husband talk to you about it. The situation is getting out of control . . . we can't manage our son anymore."

"I totally understand! I am young too and I used to do things that I regretted afterwards. But I am glad that I knew Jesus even though I was doing wrong things. Also, my father and my mother were there to discipline me any time I did something wrong. And . . . of course, their prayers really helped me too. I am sure that, what Jesus can do for me, He can do it for anyone," I commented.

"Yes, if your God can change my husband, James, I believe that He can change anyone. Jean d'Or—to tell you the truth—I have a tough husband to deal with. But, God is good; He is saving our marriage. Meeting you was a blessing. You appeared as an angel, sent to us from heaven," Janette spoke with emotion.

"Let's thank God for that!" I said.

"Yes, He deserves praise. I have tried so many times to get my husband to go to church; but he always resisted because he would say that the pastors just wanted his money and that he was not interested in giving to them. Can you imagine somebody thinking that way?" Janette said.

"I don't blame him. Most people—especially successful people—think that way because some pastors do preach about money, talk about money and ask for money. I don't mean all pastors; but, some of them do. I grew up in a church in Africa where some of the pastors were obsessed with money. I recall that one of them used to point out the amount that every Christian member had to bring into the church. The more activities you were involved in, the more money you would have to pay. They put it in a way that made you feel guilty. It was really outrageous!"

"Then, what happened if you didn't have money to bring?" Janette asked.

"You wouldn't be able to continue doing your activities in the church until you were able to bring the money. Believe me, it was ridiculous."

"It sounds that way . . . I have never heard of such a thing! I have heard a few pastors on TV asking for money, but they never went that far. Is it still the same there or have things changed?" Janette said.

"Well, during phone-time with my mother, she said similar things were still happening in different ways. But, not all churches and not all pastors are like that. Again, it could be just one pastor who is misrepresenting the church or the group," I said.

"Yes, that's a good way to look at it. God has blessed you with wisdom. I am so proud of you!" Janette said.

"Since I joined my church that I attend here in Canada, I have learned different things. They don't really talk about money. As Christians, we know that we have to bring some of the blessing into the house of the Lord. It's obvious that God blesses us so we can bless and support His work. But, when it goes beyond, it becomes disturbing."

"So, what do you think about those pastors who preach otherwise?" Janette asked.

"Well, the Bible says that we will be judged according to the content of our knowledge. And . . . "Not everyone who cries out God's name will go to heaven.' It is bad news for hypocrites who cry out falsely . . . and also those who deliver false messages."

"So what about those who know nothing about God?" Janette asked.

"They will still be judged—but differently. That is up to God as to how He will look at them. However, it is clear enough that Jesus will not return before everyone knows or hears the gospel. Believe me, one day everyone will hear the good news about salvation. That's one of our duties as Christians—to deliver good news to everyone on earth. Trust me, it will be even worse for those who hear the good news of salvation and still play ignorant."

"Fair enough. I'm so glad that my husband is going to go to church now," Janette said.

"Oh, Jean d'Or, here is James. Please, talk to him. It was a pleasure talking to you again. I look forward to seeing you tomorrow. I hope we are still going . . . hm, I don't know . . . talk to James. I think he is changing our schedule. He just gave me a funny look when I mentioned tomorrow's appointment," Janette said with a smile.

"Thank you Janette; it was also my pleasure talking to you again. There is a lot more to discuss about God . . . there's much to learn. Yes, let me talk to James and see what he says. I hope we can still make it for tomorrow. If not, then we'll meet next week," I replied.

Janette was waiting to hand the phone to James; but, there was shouting coming from a different room where James and his son were arguing.

"James, James . . . Jean d'Or is on the phone waiting to talk to you!" Janette shouted.

"I'll be right there. Let's go. I want you to hear this," James' voice came from another room.

"Hello my Christian friend. Sorry, but I've been dealing with this situation with my son. Believe me, he is a trouble–maker. I am going to put you on speaker phone so both of us can hear you. Is that okay?" James asked.

"Yes, it's fine. Everybody can be a bit difficult sometimes," I replied.

"Yeah, but this one is the champion," James sighed.

"Yes, and I learned it all from you, Dad!" his son argued with him.

"Oh yeah! Well, let's see where you are going to get the money to blow now? I am not going to give you any more money and I will make sure no one else does—not even your mother," James responded angrily.

The argument continued. "Stop it, both of you!" Janette shouted.

I decided to speak up; I asked James to take the phone so that I could talk to him privately.

"James . . . remember that we move forward not backward. You have accepted Jesus; so, why don't you show your Son the goodness of God too. The only way to do it is to forgive him and show him that you love him as God loves us. Teach him and help him to change," I urged.

"Do you know what he says all the time?" James blurted.

"No, what does he say?" I asked.

"He says that 'the law is there to be broken" . . . can you imagine that? I thought I was bad; but, my son is worse and he needs more discipline and lessons than I do. I think it would take a whole church, full of pastors, to convince my son to change. Trust me, he is as evil as Satan himself," James complained.

"What exactly did he do to deserve that kind of description?" I asked.

"Too much to tell . . . it would take me a whole day. The boy has been caught so many times drinking, driving, and smoking marijuana in the car with his friends. Today was the same. I am glad that his driver's license is suspended for two years. He just cost me a lot of money to get him out of police custody. He is too much to handle. He was kicked out of school because of his bad behaviour . . . he won't be accepted by any high school anymore.

I even tried to send him to Italy to live with his grandparents and to finish his high school there; but it didn't work out. He can't even keep a job. I tried to hire him myself; but, he just goofs off."

"Where does he get the money if he is not working?" I asked.

"Jean d'Or—he is my only son. All I have will eventually belong to him. He gets the money from both sides; his grandparents, on my side and my wife's side, give him money."

"I honestly feel, James, that you have spoiled him. He will never grow up if you don't give him a chance to learn and grow. My dad was a very caring and loving father, but he didn't tolerate any wrongdoing. I remember turning 17 years old! I was involved in drinking and caused a car accident. My father was happy that everyone was okay but he refused to help me pay for the damages that I caused to the other party. At that time, I had a small transportation business; so, I was held responsible for paying for all the damage that I caused. The only way he would help me was with my business capital—and that was on the condition that I did well in school."

"I wish I could be like that. But my son isn't that smart. The only thing I have noticed that he does really well is spend! He really knows how to spend, Jean d'Or!"

"Maybe it's because he has too much money to spend. If he didn't have it, then he would not be a good spender," I commented.

"Dad . . . you used to do the same when you were my age; so, give me a break! I am just trying to enjoy my life as you did when you were a teenager. Please stop being jealous!" his son argued from the background.

"Being jealous of what? Look at you now! You can't even put your life together. Believe me, if you don't get yourself together, you won't get any inheritance!" James practically shouted.

"Oh yeah? Well, Mom will give me hers. You can keep yours—I don't need it!" he shouted back.

"James . . . what's your son's name?" I asked.

"Oliver," James replied.

So I asked James to put me back on the speaker phone, so that I could talk to his son.

"Oliver? Can I say something since you both have included me in this?" I asked.

"Yeah! What's up?" Oliver said with an angry voice.

"I know you may not believe in the Bible but remember that you are talking to your father. That means you should show him respect. You may not understand where he is coming from but, believe me, he knows what you are going through. He's been there, done that. So he is trying to protect you because he loves you more than you can even imagine. He just paid your bail . . . none of your friends would have done that. All they could have done was say 'sorry' and left you there. But when your father heard you had been arrested, he rushed to come and get you out of there. That's what we call love and forgiveness—regardless of your mistakes. So you should give him credit for that," I said.

"Whatever, buddy," Oliver replied impolitely.

"Yes—whatever that means—but he still has your back. So you should apologize and make things right. Maybe you should join your mother and father who are in the process of changing their lives," I urged.

"Do you think my dad will ever change? If he does, then I will too," Oliver responded.

Our conversation continued back and forth; but, by this time, it was getting very late. I asked Oliver to pick up the phone so I could talk to him alone.

"Oliver, please apologize to your family. They love you more than you can imagine; I have noticed that already. I know that they would be so happy if you do it."

"No man . . . my dad should be the one to apologize! Did you hear the way he was shouting at me?"

"Your dad is your father. Go ahead and see what happens."

He put the phone back on speaker and began, "I'm not good at making apologies . . . but here goes," he paused for a moment. "I am sorry, Mom and Dad; I will try my best to change and to be a good son," Oliver spoke in a quiet manner.

"We would like to see that," James said calmly.

"So . . . no more shouting at me, right?" Oliver asked.

"If you change—yes," James promised.

So I asked James and Janette to come to the phone so that Oliver wouldn't be able to hear what I was going to say to them.

"James . . . shouting every single time isn't helping at all. The more you shout, the more children get used to it. And it only becomes troubling to you, not your children. In the end, you lose your temper and it never actually changes your son's behaviour. I remember that my father could go for years and years without losing his temper; but, when he did, I paid attention! I knew that it meant that something had to be changed right away. I don't know if you have read or heard about Jesus when he got angry in the Temple; He made a whip and threw tables over. Everyone paid attention and ran out. For the three and one–half years that Jesus taught, He lost His temper only a few times. I suggest that you lose your temper only when it's necessary. And I think you should take a moment and show Oliver that you love him."

James and Janette both expressed that it was surprising to see Jesus in that kind of situation.

"Thank you Jean. We don't know what to say to you. Thanks be to God for bringing you into our lives," Janette spoke sincerely.

"Jean d'Or . . . I think we may not be able to make it to church tomorrow. Besides that . . . I was thinking that you could come here in the evening, maybe at dinner–time, so that you can meet with our son. He really needs someone like you; but, you don't have to do it if you don't feel comfortable about it. I believe you may be able to help him," James added.

"You mean come over tomorrow and talk to him?" I asked.

"My son lives out-of-town; so, he will be gone tomorrow. But, he said that he would come back to meet with you on Tuesday evening."

"No problem, James . . . I'd love to. I will look forward to meeting you as a family," I added.

"Thank you so much for doing that," James said.

"Please don't thank me. I am just God's servant, trying to complete His mission on earth. All the thanks should go to Him alone!" I said.

I remembered that my first mid-term exam was on Tuesday evening. 'What's more important—to save someone's lost soul or to get a good mark on my midterm?' I decided that I would rather bring one lost soul to God through Jesus' salvation.

"Since you are familiar with downtown Toronto . . . let's meet at the same place we were supposed to meet tomorrow; then, you can follow me. What about 4:00 p.m.?" James asked.

"Yes, that sounds perfect to me. James . . . can we pray together before we go?" I asked.

"Yes, let's do it. Let me call everyone over and put you on speaker so we can all participate," James replied.

'Wow, he is getting bolder,' I thought.

"Please go ahead . . . we are all here," Janette said.

I prayed for everyone, including Oliver, who I had yet to meet in person.

"Amen," they all responded.

"See you on Tuesday, Jean d'Or," James said.

"I can't wait," I replied.

We ended the call and I went to my bedtime prayers and thanked God for another opportunity that He was opening for me to talk and teach His word and show His mercy. It was a special moment—a moment when I felt the presence of God within me. Then, I told myself: '*If I can feel it, I can talk about it and, if I can talk about, then I can do it. This is my time to glorify His name.*'

Possibilities in God

It's funny how time goes slowly when you are very excited about something you are going to do, somewhere you are going to go, or people you are going to see. I had been praying and reading some helpful chapters in the Bible and other books to get myself ready for Tuesday's meeting. It was Monday and I was already counting the hours; but, I also kept thinking about my midterm exam. So, I decided to send an email to my professor about the possibility of missing the exam. I knew that my professor was a Christian too; so, there was a good chance that she would understand. I felt that life was too short to worry about something like this. At least I was doing the right thing for my God. This was a once-in-a–lifetime opportunity!

So, I emailed my teacher about my absence on Tuesday. I knew that I was taking a risk; but, I knew it would be worth it. God is good and He has a way of working things out. A couple of hours later, my professor emailed me back and told me not to worry. They had arranged for the exam to be held in the morning instead because they did not have enough exam proctors available for the evening.

"Good luck Jean d'Or. I am so proud of you and I am certain that God is too!" my professor said in her email.

While I was studying for my midterm exam, I received a phone call. It was my friend Frank who wanted to check up on me and make certain that I was ready for my meeting with Oliver and his parents.

"Are you ready for tomorrow . . . what are you going to talk about?" Frank asked.

"I think we should talk about Jesus' salvation. We haven't talked about it yet and I think that James and Janette need to hear about it," I said.

"Good point. Remember what your dad told you; when you are talking to people about the gospel, don't start with the negative but with good things they have done. Give them encouragement . . . then talk about how they can change and do even better with God's help. Show them that Jesus Christ is the one and only way to reach God and make it into heaven," Frank advised.

"Yes Frank . . . I do remember what my father told me . . . thanks for reminding me. I will definitely call you after our meeting," I replied.

We hung up and I went back to my studies. As the time for my exam approached, I thought about how amazing how God is and He can make the impossible possible. Earlier, I had been worried about my midterm exam; but, God took care of it. I breezed through the exam easily, although it was very difficult. That afternoon, I got ready for my meeting with James and his son. I felt that I should carry an extra Bible to give as a gift to the boy. I only had one which was mine; so, I purchased a new one at a nearby bookstore before I left for Toronto.

When I arrived at our meeting point in Toronto at 3:55 p.m., James was not there yet. I was pleased because I wanted to be there first anyway. He arrived about ten minutes late.

"Hi, d'Or. I'm sorry I am late. I had to catch up on some phone calls. My son is on his way to my house," James said.

I drove behind him, following his car. As we approached his residence, I was amazed at his huge, beautiful house. At the front, there was a large gate. As we approached, the gate opened automatically . . . I guess he must have had a controller key in his car. As we parked our cars, I could not believe how grand the house looked from the outside. Then, I thought of what it must be like on the inside. It was like being in a movie!

"You can leave your car here; it's going to be safe," James said.

"Thank you," I said.

"This is our winter home," James said. "During the summer we live on the island. We stay here in the winter because it's too cold and icy to use our boat. We have to have someone living in the island home year-round though; so, we have some caretakers stay there. Some years, we also visit my parents in Italy," James explained.

"Beautiful . . . you have two homes in the same area. God has really blessed you," I said.

"Thank you, and yes we are blessed. But, I have never really felt it until we met and talked about God's blessing. I can tell you that I've never truly appreciated all that I have until now. And I am not only talking about money and possessions, but also things such as health and family. My family was falling apart; but, now it is getting back together. I guess I was the cause of everything bad that was happening in our family," James said.

"No, you are not the cause. Satan is the one who wants to destroy your family. When we give him a foothold in our life, he will try to destroy everything that is truly important. The good news is that God is taking over," I said.

Once again I wondered how people such as James could suffer the pain of not having happiness despite all the money they had. He had everything a human being dreams about, I thought. But neither he nor his family had been happy.

We walked out into the back yard of his 'winter home' and out across the dock to where James had a powerful motor boat. In moments, we were skimming over the sparkling water. Since it was my first time riding in such a beautiful boat, I really enjoyed the ride! The homes on the island that I saw were beautiful, as I had expected. Including James' home, they were quaint and pristine. They are those kinds of houses that leave remarkable memories in your mind.

"Good . . . my son is here already," James said as we approached the harbour. "You can talk and get to know each other before supper. Oliver is kind of an aggressive person, so bear with him, Jean d'Or. But . . . if you could handle me, you will be able to handle him too," James chuckled.

"What God is doing with you . . . He can do with your son as well," I said.

"Yes . . . I forgot that God is with you. I have a habit of depending on myself for everything. It will take me a while to change my habits. The important thing now is that I know God is included in my business," James said.

It made me feel better to hear James acknowledge God's power in that way. I thought of how—not long ago—he was a man who had ignored God and His people.

When we went inside, Janette and Oliver were their waiting for us. They were all nicely dressed, the dining room table was beautifully set and they welcomed me as if I was a king!

"Welcome, Jean d'Or," Janette said.

I greeted Janette and her son. "Thank you Janette. Hi Oliver . . . it's very nice to meet you. I have been looking forward to meeting you today."

"It's very nice to meet you too. My mom and dad told me so much about you and that's why I am here today," Oliver replied.

We sat down on a beautiful leather couch and looked at each other. Oliver fidgeted a bit and looked at me as if he was already expecting me to start talking. But, I took my time to settle down first and enjoy the atmosphere.

It was Janette who spoke first. "As we have told you Oliver, Jean d'Or is a very nice young man who has the ambition to work hard and to be successful. He is very spiritual and wise . . . he graduated from Bible College in the USA in 2006 and he is now in college studying business," Janette explained.

"Thank you Janette for the introduction. That's very nice of you," I replied.

"You are welcome Jean. What can we get you? We have apple juice, iced tea and more," Janette offered.

"Water is fine, thank you."

"Well . . . as you can see . . . we are surrounded with lots of water!" Janette laughed.

"No doubt about that!" I laughed in unison. "You have a beautiful home and life; you should be very grateful to God for all of this."

"I am, Jean d'Or . . . but I wish that my husband and son were more grateful. They are always complaining about things; they just don't seem to be satisfied with what they have. James is getting better at showing gratitude. But, it still makes me sad that we have so much and they cannot be happy with it," Janette said.

"I am sorry, Janette," James said. "I didn't realize what we had until I started learning about God's blessings."

"I am so glad to hear that," I said. "You know what? *Happiness doesn't come from money but from the good things that you can do with that money. Also, you will never lose money by running after God, but you will lose God by running after money.* Money isn't everything. *It's nice to have it, but it won't bring happiness if you let it control you. And if you don't have God in your life, you are in real danger that money will control you,*" I said.

"Nice . . . I'm impressed," Oliver expressed.

"What did I say?" James laughed. "See Oliver! Didn't I say you would like him?"

"Thanks," I smiled. "So tell me a little bit about yourself, Oliver. Your parents didn't say much about you. They said that you would tell me yourself."

"Excuse me; I'm going to let you boys enjoy your meeting. I've got to get the supper ready," Janette said. "Can you give me a hand?" she asked of her husband.

Both she and James got up and went into the kitchen.

Oliver stared at me for a moment. "Let's see . . . where should I start? Well, I am not Christian, for sure, and I have never been to church or read the Bible. So I am open to any challenge you bring to me. I am not in school either; but, I would like to go back and get my high school diploma so I can go to college. What about you, besides that you are Christian?" Oliver asked.

We spoke for few minutes, talking about ourselves and our backgrounds. I already knew that the family was of Italian descent; but, I discovered that it was their dream to move to Italy after James and Janette retired.

"You have mentioned that money isn't everything," Oliver said. "You say that it does not bring happiness without God in it. Then, why do people get crazy about it if it isn't all we need?"

"Good question!" I said. "People who get crazy about money are those people who are controlled by money. But, those who are controlled by God don't get crazy about money. They use their money to fulfil God's work on earth. When you don't know God or you don't have God in your heart, you have to rely on other things. It could be money, pride in one's self or any number of other things. Believe me—the way these other things can control you—it would be crazy, as you said, and you wouldn't even notice it."

"What about if you have God? Would He not control you too?" Oliver asked.

"In a way, yes. But He doesn't control you in a way that gets you crazy; loving God and serving Him brings peace and freedom. God gives us freedom to enjoy our lives. He only leads us to good things which bring success and happiness. The opposite can happen when money controls you. If you love money and have lots of it . . . this can lead to arrogance. You might think that it does not matter if you break the law because you can afford to pay the charges; so, it does not matter how you act . . .

"Yes . . . I've thought that way myself," Oliver admitted.

"When you notice that you can't control yourself, it's time to look deep down into your heart and try to find out where both your heart and mind belong. How often do you think about money? How good or bad have you become since you focused on money? Please don't get me wrong. I don't mean you only do wrong things when you have money . . . there are so many people who aren't Christians and do good things on earth. The question is—how many times do they do those good things? Are they getting rewards in heaven or just on earth because of those good things they've done? Look Oliver. If people run after money . . . money alone cannot bring happiness. They need God for fulfillment."

"So . . . what about those who don't have money?" Oliver asked.

"Those who don't have money and don't have God in their lives can also be miserable. They can blame rich people and God for their poverty. Either way, we all need God no matter how much we have in the way of material possessions. *If we allow money to control us, that's when we allow evil to lead us.*"

I continued. "I don't know if you have heard that 'the love of money is a root of all kinds of evil.'"

"I think I had; but, I have never paid much attention to it. Is it a Bible verse?" Oliver asked.

"Yes it is; it's in the book of 1 Timothy 6:10." I opened my Bible and showed him.

"This verse summarizes everything that we've been talking about. Money can become evil if you fall in love with it."

At that moment, Janette came back into the room. She put more water into my glass and set out bowls with potato chips in them.

"I can see you guys are getting along," Janette said.

"Yes, Mom, we are," Oliver replied.

"Oliver . . . now that you are learning how money can create problems . . . how do you think you are going to handle it?" I asked.

"Hm, I don't know yet. We'll see," Oliver replied.

"Exactly! You can't know how until you include God in your life. Money isn't the problem; it's the way you relate to money and the importance that you place on it. I know we all have some important goals in life. As for me, my most important priority is to place God first; that makes me happier. I believe you can find happiness in God too, Oliver."

"Jean, I hate conditions! I hate the way you have to do this or that to be a Christian. Laws don't apply to me. I like to do what I want to do, when and wherever I want to do it. It's dog-eats–dog out there; everybody wants to get even and I have to stay ahead of the pack," Oliver said with a smug voice.

"I don't blame you for thinking that way, Oliver. No one likes conditions or being told what to do. But, if you keep doing things in your own way and never listen to anyone else, there will come a time in your life when you will regret it. I know because it happened to me when I was 17 years old. I couldn't stand to listen to anyone's advice, not even my parents'. I drank and partied, drove drunk and rode with other drivers who were drunk. You know what happened? Some of my friends who I did these things with ended up getting killed. I realized that I was heading down the same path if I didn't change my ways. That's when I decided to come back to God. Since then, I've never looked back. So, I believe that you should consider your life seriously."

"I do consider my life seriously. I just never got interested in the whole God thing because I have never felt that I needed Him," Oliver said.

All this time, we had been talking about God; but, I was really hoping to get to the subject of salvation. And I wanted James and Janette to be part of that conversation because I did not believe that they had committed their lives to Christ yet.

"Oliver, we all need God in our lives. Look at your parents now—they're becoming happier and are getting along better with each other. But . . . look what just happened to you. You lost your drivers' license because of your actions. Does that not teach you a lesson?" I continued. "I need you to take a moment and think about it while we are eating our supper. You have mentioned to me that you like to be ahead of the pack. This is your opportunity to be a real leader among your friends. Show them a new style of living—show them how you can be wealthy and still glorify God."

"Fellows . . . the food is ready. Come to the table," Janette called.

We got up and went into the dining room. The table was beautifully set and everything looked wonderful.

"This looks amazing," I told the couple.

"I hope you enjoy it. Thank God, not me! Remember you said that?" Janette said smiling.

And I really did enjoy the meal that was prepared with much love and happiness.

"What did you boys talk about while we were in the kitchen?" James asked.

"We shared about our mistakes as young boys—mistakes we now regret. There was something else that I wanted to talk about; but, I was waiting until you two could be part of the conversation."

"And what is that about?" Janette said.

"It's about salvation."

"Salvation?" James repeated.

"Yes, Jesus' salvation . . . how Jesus made a big impact in our lives by taking our place on the cross. Please, let's eat and we will talk about it later. You both have worked too hard on this lovely meal to let it get cold. And knowing me—once I start talking about it, I won't want to stop," I chuckled.

"Sounds good," James said.

During our meal, we talked about my school and my goals; we also talked about their lives and what they planned to do in the future. After dessert, Oliver and I cleared the table and put the dishes in the dishwasher; then, we moved back into the living room to talk about salvation. Once we had settled, I started by taking out my Bible and handing the new one to Oliver. "Here . . . hang on to this one for now," I said.

"Oh thanks, but I don't know how to use it," Oliver said.

"Don't worry—we are going to help each other."

I asked Janette and James if they had Bibles and discovered that they had only one; so they would have to share.

"Sorry, I never carry a Bible on me," James said. "But I am going to get one . . . soon."

"It's ok. I don't mind sharing," Janette said with a smile.

I asked them to open their Bible to John 3:16—21; I helped Oliver to find the verse since it was the first time that he had ever opened a Bible. I was so happy to see this happening!

I began to read. 'For God so loved the world that He gave His only begotten Son, that whosoever believeth in Him should not perish, but have everlasting life.' After reading these verses, I went into deep explanations on how one who believes in Jesus is not condemned as opposed to who does not believe yet—and also touched a little bit on how some people loved darkness rather than light, because their deeds were not acceptable to God.

"The Bible tells us that we have all sinned and need to be saved from condemnation, and that salvation comes only through Jesus Christ because he died on the cross," I explained.

"Why is it like that? Why through Jesus . . . not straight to God?" Oliver asked.

I willingly responded to Oliver. "It is through Jesus Christ because he was the only one who could take the punishment for our sins. Because of Him, we don't really have to do anything . . . except to accept that we have sinned against God by doing wrong. We have to welcome Him into our hearts and let Him change our lives. We have to stop engaging in behaviour that we know is wrong and allow Him to lead us."

"Why did he have to die? Was that necessary?" James asked. "Didn't God have the power to save the world? After all, he created it. I don't understand this verse. If God is as powerful as we hear, why could He not just change things around?"

"God makes it pretty clear in the Bible that the punishment for sin is death. So, yes . . . someone had to die for our sins. Without Jesus, we only had death to look forward to; but, because he paid the price for us, we have a choice. God gave us two choices: 'Life and death, the blessing and the curse.' Sometimes, it seems that men are attracted to anything which brings darkness."

"Is that really in the Bible? I have never heard of that," James said.

"Yes it is . . . let's open our Bible to Deuteronomy 31:19-20." I gave them time to find the verse before reading. 'I call heaven and earth to witness against you today, that I have set before you life and death, the blessing and the curse. So choose life in order that you may live, you and your descendants, By loving the LORD your God, by obeying His voice, and by holding fast to Him; for this is your life and the length of your days, that you may live in the land which the LORD swore to your fathers, to Abraham, Isaac, and Jacob, to give them.' "So you see . . . God has already promised us a good life and gave a choice and recommendation to choose life."

"That is making more sense now," James said.

"Most of us don't know that a good life has been given to us on earth and that it is up to us whether to choose it or not. The only condition God made is to obey His voice and put him first. Imagine! Just obey and you get to live an ideal life. You can't get any better than that. How many people would offer that? Maybe some parents," I added with a smile.

I could see that I had their attention, so I continued. "And it is sad that humankind was deceived into disobeying God. That's how we became sinners in the first place. The only way to redeem us was for God to shed the blood of His only son who had never sinned. And everyone who accepts this will be saved and not perish."

"What a love!" Janette spoke with emotion.

"Yes . . . what a love!" I said.

"So God has a child? I mean a son?" Janette asked.

"Good question Janette. Jesus is God's first word spoken and the word created everything. The Bible says that: 'Jesus is the word and the word lives in God.' We are created in God's image and that's why Jesus calls us 'my brothers and sisters' because we live in God with him when we choose to follow him. You can read these Bible verses yourselves in John 1:1-14."

"Thank you . . . I will," Janette said.

"My point is—if Jesus could obey God by coming down and leaving everything in heaven to die for us—why can't you accept His gift and make those good choices that lead to happiness in life?"

"What if God does not exist?" Oliver asked.

"Then you lose nothing. As a matter of fact, you gain everything by fully controlling your life and living a happy and successful one," I paused; then, I continued. "You know, Oliver . . . success equals happiness; if you are not happy with what you have; then, you are far away from successful. I can also tell you this: *having money, cars, houses and all you want does not make you fulfilled unless you are happy with it.* So, when you can't find that happiness in your achievement, then you need to look elsewhere. Look to see what you are missing in your life. I am certain that you have tried everything to satisfy your heart. The question is—are you happy enough?"

"Not really," Oliver replied.

"I like your honesty. Let me ask you a question. How much money do you spend just for the weekend? I mean, going out into bars, night clubs and so on . . ."

"Maybe thousands," Oliver replied.

"Unbelievable! And how much do you pay just to get into the bars or clubs?"

"It depends really; some clubs charge $50 t0 $100 just for the cover. Why are you getting into this?"

Janette fidgeted upon hearing this. She clearly was unhappy with how Oliver had been spending his money.

"My point is that you are paying $100.00 just to get into clubs, where evil things are done, while you pay nothing to go to church where Holy things are happening. You can save your money by going to Church and you won't have to worry about getting hurt or having something bad happen to you. You could find other ways to use your money that would bring you greater success and happiness," I continued. "Going back to your question about God's existence—you really lose nothing by believing in someone who brings love, happiness, and success to your life. Try Him and see what He will do for you."

"Ok, I guess you and God win. I'll try. So . . . what do I need to do?" Oliver asked.

"You need to admit that you are a sinner and welcome Jesus as your saviour into your heart."

"Okay," Oliver said.

I asked Oliver to repeat after me while I recited a forgiveness prayer. I also prayed for comfort and protection for the whole family. It was a tremendous moment for me and the whole family. Everyone had tears in their eyes, including me.

We read a couple of verses from the Bible and discussed what it means to be a Christian. Then I decided to give Oliver and his parents some homework. I jotted down a few verses. We read and explored them together. Then, I asked them to meditate on each verse throughout the week.

"I would like to recommend these verses; please mark them down and read them throughout the week." I outlined the verses to them:

♦ about our sins: Romans 3:23-24 'For all have sinned and fall short of the glory of God being justified as a gift by His grace through the redemption which is in Christ Jesus.' And Romans 3:10 'there is none righteous, not even one.'
♦ about God's answer for sin: Romans 6:23 'for the wage of sin is death, but the free gift of God is eternal life in Christ Jesus our Lord.' And John 1:12 'But as many as received Him, to them He gave the right to become children of God, even to those who believe in His name.'
♦ about our response to God's salvation: 1 John 1:9 'If we confess our sins, He is faithful and righteous to forgive us our sins and to cleanse us from all unrighteousness.' And Romans 10: 13 'Whoever will call on the name of the Lord will be saved.'

After reading these verses, I invited Oliver to join us on Saturday for our group meeting.

"Oh no . . . I can't make it this Saturday. I promised my friends that I'd take them boat–riding. Maybe another time," Oliver announced.

"What if there is no other time?" I asked.

"What do you mean?" Oliver asked.

"What I mean is that every week we have a different topic that we talk about. So, this might be the night that could really change your life. I think we will be talking about 'Living the Christian Life.' This would be a good one for you to hear. The boat ride will always be there."

Oliver was still adamant and did not want to give up a day with his friends, despite the urging of his parents.

"Mom, Dad—I am sure there will be another time."

"Look . . . I do understand you have priorities; but, *good opportunities don't wait for you.* What you have here is an opportunity to learn more about God and be an example to your friends as well," I stressed. "Oliver . . . remember that time runs fast and never comes back! There is a moment when we get the opportunity in life and we waste the precious time that has been given to pursue the precious opportunity offered on things that can be done later. This is a life–time opportunity that you don't want to let pass by."

"Ok, I will come," Oliver sighed. "And maybe even some of my friends will follow me. But they may need to hear it from you first. I will tell them that I have accepted Jesus . . . but you need to explain it to make them believe it more," Oliver said.

"I'd love to! Just let me know when and I will make time for that," I said.

"Thank God! We need to celebrate this wonderful moment," James spoke with emotion.

He went into the basement and grabbed a bottle of mineral water.

"Let's cruise on the water . . . it's such a beautiful evening!" James exclaimed.

We all agreed to the excursion. As we toured around the island, we discussed how lives were changing. It was God's miracle!

Although I was having a wonderful evening, I did not want to stay too long as I still had another exam to write the following day.

"I need to get back home. I have an exam tomorrow morning that I still need to study for," I said.

"It was wonderful having you as our guest," Janette replied.

They dropped me off at their other house where I had left my car. Before I left, they hugged me closely with much love. When I arrived home, I called Frank and told him the good news—that the family had all accepted Jesus and that I invited Oliver to join us at our meetings.

"By the way—can you ask Valerie to possibly touch on something else since I spoke about salvation today? Do you think she would mind talking about how to live the Christian life?"

"No problem—I'll ask her," Frank replied.

"And I was thinking—instead of going hiking at Thomas's property—maybe we can go hiking around Niagara–on–the–Lake before the real winter weather hits us. What do you think?"

"Good idea! I will let everyone know about your proposal and see what they think. I'll let you know by Thursday evening what we have decided to do."

We praised God together and ended the call. Then I thought: *'If you don't do it, you won't know the feeling of it.'*

Living the Christian Life

The group had decided to accept my idea of going hiking in Niagara-on-the–Lake. It was mid-October but still a beautiful, warm and sunny day to enjoy the outdoors. James and Janette had offered to pick me up; so, I was waiting for them outside my apartment.

"Hi, Jean d'Or, how are you?" Oliver asked as their car pulled up.

"Great . . . thank you. How is everyone here?" I asked.

"Fine . . . we're all doing fine," James replied.

I got in the car and we drove to a tourist information centre which was our meeting point in Niagara–on-the–Lake. Frank and his wife Valerie were there already; I had never known them to be late. They were always on time, which was a good example for me. I had always made excuses for being late; by getting to know Frank and Valerie, my thinking on this matter had been challenged. They really helped me to consider how respecting timing and schedules was actually a show of respect for others. It was hard in the beginning to change my habits; but, I had to do it so that I would not miss the opportunity for self–development.

"Sorry we are late," I apologized.

"Don't worry about it; you are here now. As a matter of fact, some have not arrived yet. It's just us and Thomas so far; he just stepped inside the building to get some information," Frank said.

"Who do we have here?" Frank asked as he looked directly at Oliver with a smile.

"Oh, this is Oliver. He is James' and Janette's son—the one I told you about," I replied.

Frank extended his hand to Oliver.

"Hello Oliver. It's a pleasure to meet you. Welcome," Frank said.

"Thank you. It's my pleasure to be here as well," Oliver replied.

When Thomas stepped out from the information centre, the others arrived at the same time.

"Oh, we are late; sorry guys," Mark said.

"Don't worry about it. It's just hiking and we have plenty of time today," Frank responded.

I introduced Oliver to everyone and told them about how we had met and what had happened.

"Welcome Oliver. God is happy for you and we are too," William said.

While the James and Janette were speaking to Frank, William turned and whispered, "I think we should celebrate! I am sure that God and the angels are celebrating in heaven for this family."

"That should be a good party! Let's do it today after hiking," Valerie said softly.

So, we planned a surprise celebration for James, Janette, and Oliver when we were finished.

"Let's go down to the lake—I want to touch the water," Frank said.

"This is a very nice way to exercise; I like it," Janette said.

"Yes, it is. Expect at least three hours for the hike. And be very careful; those stairs are a bit steep," I said.

While we were walking down toward the lake, Thomas started the conversation.

"How was the church you and our new group members went to on Sunday?" Thomas asked.

"We weren't able to go; but, we plan to go this Sunday," I said.

"Which church are you taking them to?" Valerie asked.

"We will need to visit a few churches before they can make a decision about which one they want to join," I said.

"That's a good idea," Valerie replied.

We continued hiking down towards the water. Some members of the group took photos while others sat on some of the large rocks and enjoyed the scenery and the conversation. It took us an hour to reach the water.

"I am so tired; I haven't done this for a long time," Janette said.

After a short break, we headed back.

"Good decision to come here Jean d'Or! I had a great time. Now I feel like a cold, refreshing drink," Frank said.

When we arrived back at our starting point, we decided to take a slow drive along the Niagara Parkway. While hiking, we had been able to have several quick and private discussions in which we agreed that we would celebrate our friends' salvation at the revolving restaurant at the Skylon Tower in Niagara Falls. Thomas had been able to slip away for a few minutes during the hike to call on his cell phone for a reservation. Fortunately, the restaurant was not busy and we did not have to wait. We also got the star treatment because one of the managers on duty that day was a former student of Thomas. As soon as we got there, we were welcomed. We were escorted to a table and had a panoramic view of Niagara Falls. The table's location was very private. I guess we were seated in the VIP area because no other people were close to us. On our way in, a few people noticed Pastor Mark and came by our table to shake his hand.

The waitress brought us menus and we ordered our food.

"We are very pleased to celebrate this evening with our new friends," Frank said while the server was pouring some water into our glasses.

"Who are we celebrating for?" James asked.

"For you and your family, James," Frank replied.

"That's nice of you; you did not have to do this. Please allow me to cover the bill. We should be the ones to thank you," James insisted.

"No sir! It is our tradition to celebrate when something good happens to one of our friends. We usually do this to support each other. So today is your turn. Sit back, relax, and enjoy," Mark said.

It was indeed wonderful to enjoy the amazing view! The conversation which followed was both warm and inviting.

"What do you do for a living, Janette and James?" Valerie asked.

"James owns several businesses and I help him manage the office. We have contractors across Canada, the USA, and Italy," Janette replied.

"How is it going?" Valerie asked.

"It's going well now that we have God in our lives. Before that, it was difficult because of the family problems that we were having. But now we really appreciate each other so much more and it makes it so much better to work together. We realize that becoming a Christian isn't easy; it's a work in progress. We also hope that our son continues to consider putting God first in his life," Janette said.

"Don't hope. All you need to do is to pray and believe. God will make it happen if you believe it," Valerie said.

The way that Valerie was directing the conversation, it occurred to me that she was trying to open up the topic of her lesson for the day.

"I was thinking today of taking this opportunity to talk about maintaining a good life as Christians," Valerie said. "There are things that we can do as Christians that will help us to grow in our faith. These include:

1. praying daily,
2. praising and worshiping God,
3. fasting, and
4. reading the Bible."

Oliver spoke for the first time. "Do you really have to fast? I don't have a problem with praying . . . praising; but, fasting—isn't that hard?"

"Yes . . . there are times we need to fast as Christians. But let's talk about praying first. Through Jesus Christ, we have access to the throne of God. In the Old Testament, animal sacrifices were offered by the high priest for full access to God. But today we are free. We don't have to offer the lambs. The Lamb of God is Jesus Christ who has taken away our sins when he died on the cross. All we need to do is to believe that Jesus is the mediator between God and us. So, when we pray to God, we should always know that, in order to reach God, we have to go through Jesus Christ. Through regular prayer, it helps us to maintain our relationship with God," Valerie explained, then continued.

"The more we pray, the more we welcome God's spirit to lead us and the more we open the heavenly door of blessings. It is also important to pray with other believers. Jesus himself recommended this in Mathew 18:19 which states: 'Again I say unto you that if two of you shall agree on earth as touching anything that they shall ask, it shall be done for them of my Father which is in heaven.'"

As Valerie paused, the manager herself came to the table along with the chef carrying our plates. She spoke to each one of us regarding the plates we had ordered.

"I do hope that you enjoy your meal," she expressed to us all.

"Thanks, we will, Helene," Thomas said.

"I am going to let you enjoy your meal and will be back later. Is there anything else you need at the moment?" she asked.

"We are fine, thanks," Valerie replied.

We were being taken care of so well. And to be served by the manager . . . I'd never experienced this treatment! When the food arrived, it was incredible! After the meal, our waitress presented us with a cake for the celebration. I had a hunch that the cake was Frank's doing.

"Valerie, we can't wait to hear the rest of your lesson," William said.

Valerie was almost finished her dessert. "I guess I can go on while you all enjoy your cake," Valerie said.

"My second point is about praising and worshiping God. Praise is an expression of admiration. It's a way of showing the feelings that we have inside by honouring or exalting someone. Worship, on the other hand, happens when we honour someone or something above all else. Praising and worshipping God is one way to express our thanksgiving to Him. It's a way of showing God how much we love and adore Him," Valerie continued.

"We should not worship anyone other than God our creator. We have seen many human beings give praise to another human being for things accomplished. But, if we allow anyone or anything other than God to become first in our lives, it is a form of worship and it is wrong. If a human being is willing to praise . . . that person should only praise and worship God for His blessings."

After a brief pause, Valerie resumed her lesson. "We can find many verses in the Bible about praising and worshiping God. One of my favourites is John 4:24. It says: 'God is a Spirit: and they that worship Him must worship Him in spirit and in truth.' I also really like Philippians 2:11 which states: 'And that every tongue should confess that Jesus Christ is Lord, to the glory of God the Father.' Every tongue means that everyone on earth should praise God. There is no exception. It does not say only the poor because they struggle to survive or only the rich—but everyone. I love it!" she spoke with feeling.

Then she continued. "When we are talking about praise and worship, we are also talking about thanksgiving. We can praise God by giving thanks to Him for all the opportunities that we are given. We can give back to the communities and people who are really in need of His blessings and make His name known around the world because of the good things we do with His blessings. His name will be praised because of that."

"So can we praise and worship Jesus Christ too?" James asked.

"Yes! God is described as three persons in one; when we praise Him, we acknowledge the Father, Son and Holy Ghost. 1 John 5:7 says: 'For there are three that bear record in heaven: the Father, the Son, and the Holy Ghost: and these three are one.' Sometimes, we feel the need to express our praise to the Father, to Jesus Christ or to the Holy Spirit. It depends on the moment. Here is another scripture that supports this. 2 Peter 3:18 says: 'But grow in grace, and in the knowledge of our Lord and Saviour Jesus Christ. To Him is glory both now and forever. Amen.' This verse is said in worship of Jesus Christ as well," Valerie replied.

Janette spoke in a sincere manner. "I think we should even praise Him more because we are more blessed than many others," Janette commented.

"I agree, Janette. And, there are many ways you can praise and worship God. As you stay close to Him, He reveals Himself to you; a good way to stay close to Him is through prayer."

The waitress returned. "Would anyone like coffee or tea?" she asked.

After everyone placed their order, we gave praise to God for the things He had done in our lives.

Thomas spoke out with sincerity and heart. "I praise God for giving me the opportunity to be alive today. I can remember a time when I was growing up that I didn't care about anything or anybody—not even myself. My parents were upset by my bad behaviour; but, they felt helpless! The moment I received Jesus Christ as my saviour, everything changed. I was able to identify good and bad. I was able to go back to school and get my high school diploma and then go to college. It wasn't easy; but, I had to do it for my future. My parents were very sick with terminal cancer and they were worried about who was going to take over their farm when they were gone. They never got to see the change in my life while they were on this earth."

"I am sorry to hear about your parents," Janette said.

"It was a difficult time for me. One week after my mother's death, I was going through my parents' bedroom and I discovered something underneath the bed. It was two books . . . one was a Bible and the other was a Christian book. Guess who the author of that book was?"

"Who?" Janette asked.

"Our Mark"

"Pastor Mark?" Valerie questioned in a surprised manner.

"Yes, our Pastor Mark," Thomas replied.

"So what happened?" James asked.

"I wasn't really interested in the Bible; but the other book with Mark's signature in it attracted me. I opened the book to the middle and saw a verse that said: 'If you search, you will find' and another one that said: 'Whoever calls my name, would be saved'. I was desperate to change my life for the better. If this book was signed, I thought, perhaps my parents knew the author. Maybe they were even friends. So I looked Mark up on the website that was listed in the book and found his church address. I called the telephone number and asked the receptionist to transfer my call—but she refused. So I decided to drive over. When I got there, I introduced myself to the receptionist, told her about my recent phone call and asked her to give Mark my father's name. She came back with Mark himself who welcomed me into his office. We spoke for a while; then, he prayed for me—I was saved that day. I went back home happier than ever before. A few years later, I got baptized in his church and he introduced me to this group. We've been friends ever since. I give praise to God for changing my life and forgiving all my sins," Thomas testified.

"What a transformation!" Janette exclaimed.

"What were you doing before being a Christian?" Oliver interjected.

"It's a funny thing . . . I can't really remember what I was doing. You know, when you live a life of sin, it's hard to remember anything good about it. You always remember the bad parts. Even your friends don't remember the good things you did for them . . . only the bad things you have done. Those sins always come back to bite you! Truly, *you live a life of blindness when you don't know the truth.*"

"That's true," I said.

Thomas went further with his personal testimony. "I praise God for saving my life—now I am a changed man. I get to enjoy my life fully. Back then, I couldn't even think of getting married. My girlfriend left me because I couldn't commit to her alone. To me, it seemed to be a good life; but, believe me, it was hell! I wasted my parents' money on worthless things. My so-called friends back then nick-named me 'Big Money Spender' because I didn't care about prices. If I wanted it, I would buy it—no matter what. Now I can identify good and bad. The Bible has become my favourite book to read. God is good and I will worship him with all I have for the rest of my life."

After Thomas' testimony, the waitress came back and poured more coffee, tea, and water into our glasses.

Before Valerie went back to her lesson, I made a comment about Thomas' testimony. "You know everyone . . . I believe God works in ways that no one can fully understand. I have learned that God uses righteous people to save lost people's souls or to bless others so that they can testify. When I think about how my father and I were kidnapped, how my father was killed and how I was able to escape the kidnapping, I can't help but wonder about God's purpose in all of this. Here I am testifying about God's love today. I am sometimes sad that my father is not here to see it; but, then I remember that he is with God—enjoying his reward—and I am certain that he is proud of me . . . looking down and saying: 'You are doing well; keep up the good work . . . God and I are happy for you!'"

"Thanks Thomas and Jean d'Or for the beautiful testimony and devotional words; I can only imagine how happy you are now!" Valerie said. "Let's continue our study. My third point is about fasting—why we fast, where and when is it good to fast and how we should do it."

Valerie continued. "Some of you know that I used to be a volunteer missionary in a few countries in Africa. The way that the African people pray, praise and worship God is totally different from the way we do it here in North America. They spend more time praying and praising than most of us do. Some individuals fast weekly and churches do it on a monthly schedule."

"So why do we have to fast if Jesus died for us?" Oliver asked.

"Good question Oliver! . . . Jesus died for our sins so that we won't be condemned; but Jesus fasted for two reasons:

1. Jesus fasted for himself in order to have more strength to face the battle which he was about to face on the cross. This was not an easy act; so, he needed more heavenly power and encouragement to be able to complete his mission.
2. Jesus fasted to set a good example for us and to show us how to reach God by praying and fasting."

Valerie extended her wisdom. "Fasting has been a tradition in Judaism and Christianity as well as other faiths. Jesus himself fasted for 40 days and 40 nights. We can read about fasting in the Old Testament as well as in the New. The act of fasting boosts the power of our prayers. It helps to intensify our faith in an area where it may be lacking. So the reason we fast is that it is a way to increase the power of our faith."

"I guess it's necessary to do it then," Oliver said.

"Yes it is. Let's talk about where and when it is good to fast. We can do it in our own home by taking a day off and basically do nothing but pray. If it is organized, we can fast in cell groups or in the Church. However, it seems that we can't afford to have a free day without being too occupied nowadays. Therefore, we all must take some time on the weekend or if we have a day off during the week. The key is to know what you are fasting for. You can't just fast because it's a tradition; it should be for something specific, such a request that you want to submit to God. These requests could be for things such as greater faith, for peace in the world, or healing. You can choose a few hours, a whole day or several days until you feel your request is accepted."

"So, this means that you can't eat or drink anything?" James asked.

"In some countries in Africa, I noticed that they don't eat at all when they are fasting," Valerie answered.

I took the opportunity to participate. "Yes, I remember fasting three days straight with no food at all. We might have had water if needed. And it was done weekly."

"Is it because you didn't have enough food or because you were in a civil war and needed peace?" Oliver asked.

"No, Oliver. It's not about food; but, yes . . . I remember a lot of people were fasting and praying for peace," I replied.

"So, how many times do you do it now?" Oliver asked.

"Good question. I don't do it as often as I used to. And I feel different in a spiritual way. Back then, I could pray for healing and see the results right way. Now, sometimes I see the result and other times I don't. It depends on God's will and timing," I said.

"So what makes you not fast now?" Oliver asked me.

"I didn't say I don't do it. I just don't practice it the way that I used to. But I still fast. I think that the environment and comfort that we enjoy here in North America has a big impact. We have all we need here and we almost forget what we as Christians should do when it comes to fasting. We don't see any need for it until we are in trouble," I said.

Valerie picked up again with her point of view. "That's right; we need to fast to increase our power of faith in our prayers. I call that 'sacrifice'. How should we do it? As I said, in Africa and third world countries, fasting is a regular part of Christian life. They can do it for a full day or several days at a time. On our side of the world—we need to learn how to fast. If there is something that we feel that we can't live without, then we should fast from it. But, we should also spend quality time praying. We need to bring this back into our lives as Christians."

"You mean that you can set the hours that you want to fast?" Janette asked.

"Yes . . . pick a day and time to start and finish. Decide whether you are going to go without food completely or only limit yourself to certain things. Make that time count in your Christian life."

As Valerie spoke, we all felt touched. I couldn't remember the last time I had fasted and gone deeply into prayer with my God. I felt a deep hunger to spend that quiet time with Him once again.

"And when you are fasting," Valerie continued, "It should stay as a private matter—between you and God."

"Good point Valerie. I am so glad I came today . . . I nearly decided not to come," Frank said.

"We are glad you came, Thomas. Seriously, this is a wakeup call to all of us as Christians," Frank said.

The waitress came back and poured more drinks into our glasses before Valerie finished up with her last point.

"We must learn about God by reading the Bible. As a newborn or long-time follower of Christ, each of us needs to know and to understand who we serve as our Lord. The only way is to learn His word through the Bible. Every detail we need to know about God and living the Christian life is found in His word."

"That's right," Pastor Mark added. "The Bible teaches everything we need to know to live a healthy, wealthy, and successful life."

"There is a Bible verse that says: 'We are deceived because we did not learn the word of God properly.' It's true; *to know history you have to study it.* Anything you want to know the facts about, you have to take time and learn about it. That tells us that, as Christians, we should read the Bible to understand what God wants for and from us and how we should live our lives to reflect His Image on earth. Prayer, praise and worship, and fasting aren't going to keep us in good shape if we don't study the word of God correctly. We have to incorporate all of these elements into our lives. Nowadays, as technology has grown, you can get the word of God through audio books, videos or webcasts. If you don't want to do all these, you still shouldn't make any excuses—just read at your own speed until you get it. There is no rush; it's the word of God. He is patient as long as you stay close to Him," Valerie concluded.

"I have a question. Do you think this newer technology is taking away from Christians the feeling of reading the Bible on their own? I mean—does it hinder them from knowing the location of each of their favourite chapters in the Bible?" I asked.

"Yes, I think so. That's one of the reasons that cell groups and Sunday schools are so important. They empower Christians to read the Bible. Churches which operate those types of activities are doing well in helping Christians to learn the word of God," Valerie replied.

I added with a personal comment. "I think about that every time I go to church. Now, all the Bible verses are projected on the screen. No one picks up a Bible or hymn book anymore—well, maybe a few still do it. I can remember that, when I was growing up, I read the whole bible through twice. The first time was a punishment from my dad because I did something wrong—about which I don't remember. The second time was because I wanted to. I wanted to do it to be fully equipped. I memorized much of scripture, including chapters and numbers; but now . . . all I can remember is how to rephrase the verses. I can't remember all the chapters' numbers anymore—not like before. When I look at myself as a long-time Christian who can't remember chapters and verses, I wonder how much more difficult it must be now for new Christians."

"I am glad that we have this group. Yes, I agree with Jean d'Or; I feel exactly the same way," Thomas said.

Valerie reacted to our opinions. "As Christians we should find a way to learn the word of God in order to strengthen our faith and knowledge. But, we can't push back technology. Yes, it has its drawbacks; but, there are also lots of advantages too. We just have to learn to use it effectively. It's the same as getting the opportunity to have lots of money; as Christians, we have to learn how to deal with money and not to let money deal with us. The Bible in Romans 12:21 says: 'Do not be overcome by evil, but overcome evil with good."

"So you're saying that the more money we have, the more good things we should do with it?" I asked.

"Exactly my point! It's hard to know that, if you are not engaged in learning the word of God. Most of the time we think that the opportunity we get is coming from our own hard work. Why do we think that way? We know how to pray for the opportunities; but, we haven't learned or read about how we should conduct ourselves when we get them. If you never read the Bible, you can never know that it is written in the book of Ephesians 6:10: 'So then, while we have opportunity, let us do good to all people, and especially to those who are of the household of the faith.' To maintain a good Christian life, we have to study the word of God constantly because His words live forever," Valerie declared.

The manager came back and asked whether she could get us anything else.

"No thank you. Everything was great though," Frank replied.

"So, what are you celebrating?" the manger asked.

"Our friends here just accepted Jesus Christ as their Saviour," Valerie said.

"You should too, if you are not already. But, you may be one of us too since you were a previous student of Thomas," James said to the manager.

The manager didn't appear to mind James' forwardness. "I am now. But, I wasn't when I was a student of his. He was a good professor; everyone in my class liked him," she replied.

"Good to hear! Can we have the bill please?" James said.

"No, no . . . I am going to take care of it," Frank intervened.

As I listened to James' rather aggressive remarks to the manager, I realized that he was still the same outspoken fellow I had encountered at the gas station. But, there was a difference . . . James was speaking with a Christian outlook. '**Just don't be too aggressive**' was a thought which entered my mind. Maybe my heart was speaking to both James and I!

There was a happy and rather jovial argument about who was going to pay the bill. I was sitting back and relaxing. Since I was with millionaires, I didn't have to worry about the bill which Frank finally won the privilege of paying.

"Let's thank God for this wonderful time he has given us today!" Pastor Mark said.

We gave a prayer for thanks and descended in the Skylon's yellow elevator.

"What are your plans for tomorrow?" Thomas asked the newfound family of friends.

"We don't know. Tomorrow is Sunday; we may go to church, but we don't know yet," James replied.

"It would be wonderful for you to go to church to give God praise. He deserves it!" Valerie commented.

We got down to ground level where we said our goodbyes to one another.

Janette approached me and touched my shoulder. "Jean d'Or—I was thinking . . . why don't you come with us and spend a night at our home so that tomorrow we can go together to that church you wanted to take us to last week?" Janette asked.

"That's a good idea. That way I can call and ask all my friends to meet him after church at our home," Oliver commented.

"I think I can do that," I said. "But I would need to go by my apartment first to pick up my church clothes, if you don't mind."

"Not at all. It's our pleasure to have you over for the night at our place," James added.

We drove to my apartment where I picked up suitable clothes and packed a small overnight bag. I couldn't believe how much love I was getting from this family. It was awesome to see how God can change attitudes!

While I was gathering a few things I needed for Sunday, I also picked one of my favourite movies and a Christian CD to give to James to listen to while he was driving. I had noticed that he liked listening to audio books about business; I thought that listening to some Christian songs would be a nice change for him. When we got to their home, they showed me the guest room where I would be staying.

"So what are you going to do right now? I have a movie we can watch if you're not too busy or too tired," I said.

"I think we can watch a movie; what is it about?" James asked.

"Have you watched 'Passion of the Christ' before?" I asked.

"Yes, but just half of it. I couldn't really finish it; it was too painful to watch. I don't think James and Oliver have ever watched it," Janette replied.

We agreed to view the heart-wrenching film. Although tears were abundant, we watched the movie to its conclusion.

"I can't believe He went through all that because of our sins. Now I know and I am sorry, Jesus," James exclaimed. His confession led us all to express our thankfulness for His ultimate sacrifice for us.

As I knelt beside the bed in prayer, my thoughts reflected on a day filled with passion, beauty, wonder and promise. The Lord quieted my mind—a peaceful sleep followed.

Walk the Talk

A change demands lots of discipline. As Christians, we watch every step we take because we are called to be ambassadors of God on earth. We watch what we say and what we do. Every step is judged by the whole world. We can make a difference in peoples' lives and in our own life when our conversations match our actions.

That Sunday, we all woke up a little early to prepare for church. As we were getting ready, James noticed that Oliver wasn't there. He looked all over the house—even in the yard for him—but he was gone. Finally, he decided to call his cell phone. After several rings, Oliver picked up the phone.

"Where are you? We looked for you everywhere and we couldn't find you," James inquired.

"Sorry Dad," Oliver replied with a tired voice.

Oliver hung up the phone. I guessed that he did this by accident because he sounded very tired.

"What? He hung up on me! I can't believe this. I think he snuck out through the window to that little girlfriend of his," James shouted with an angry voice followed by a few curse words.

James was very angry; but, his wife put her hands on his head and gently caressed him to cool him down.

"James . . . we have a visitor here. Check your language; you can't use those kinds of words anymore," Janette said with a soft voice.

"I'm calling him again!" James spoke angrily.

"Thank God for this beautiful day He has blessed us with!" I said in an effort to distract his anger.

"Amen, thank God," Janette agreed. "James . . . please be easy on him; he is trying."

When you are Christian, it means you are watched. Your actions speak more loudly than your words. So I kept quiet; but, I used God's presence to change James' mood. He waited for few minutes to cool down before he made another attempt to call his son. The phone rang and Oliver picked it up again.

"Where are you? Can't you hear me?" James asked again.

"Sorry Dad. I will be there in 30 minutes," Oliver replied.

We waited for Oliver; but, after an hour he still hadn't arrived. We had to leave in order to get to Church on time.

"I think we should go; the service is about to start. They usually begin at 10:00 a.m.," I said.

"Yes, let's go. Janette, are you ready to go? We're leaving," James said.

We decided to leave without Oliver. We got there late. The church was almost full and it was difficult to find a seat.

"I can't believe my son did this to me," James complained.

"It's alright; he will come around. Sometimes, it takes a little bit of work to change. Also it's better to change first those around you; then, it becomes easier to change yourself. So I believe that, once his friends accept Jesus as their saviour too, it will be much easier for him to come around completely. However, we need to keep him in prayer," I urged.

"You're right d'Or. I will feel happy to see my whole family agree on something for once," Janette said.

An usher came to get one of us after she had seated Janette.

"Go ahead; I'll get the next one," I said to James.

The service was almost over when James received a call from Oliver apologizing. James left the sanctuary so that he could speak with him. When we got out of the service, James was still talking to his son.

"When did you leave? You could have let us know. You're a big boy. You did not have to sneak out through your bedroom window," James said.

"I didn't want to wake you up. I'm sorry Dad."

"I thought that you were trying to change—to become a better man for the future. Don't you remember my promises to you? If you continue your ways, I don't think that I will be able to keep my promises."

"I know Dad, I know, and I am sorry. My friends texted and asked me to join them for a few minutes and it ended up being all night. Is Jean d'Or still with you?"

"Yes. Why?" James asked.

"I am bringing all my friends to meet him. I need him to help me convince them about the Christianity thing so that I can be with my friends too. Can I talk to him please?" Oliver asked.

James handed his cell phone to me to talk to Oliver.

"What's up JD'OR? Man, I am sorry for last night. My friends wanted to go out and we made a deal. If I went out with them last night, they would join me in this Christianity thing. Isn't that a great deal to you?" Oliver asked with a hopeful tone.

"No . . . it's a bad deal Oliver! *You have the power to take over the evil and not let the evil take over you.* The next time they try to make that kind of deal with you, reject it. You can change your friends and I believe in you," I replied.

"I hear you. Anyway, can we still meet up somewhere downtown? I will drive you back home after that. My friends still want to meet you," Oliver said.

"Okay. Here . . . talk to your Dad. Give him the address where you would like to meet," I said.

I handed the phone back to James and I could hear that he was getting the address from his son. He dropped me off at a restaurant where I met Oliver and his five friends, including his girlfriend.

We hugged. "We'll see you next Saturday, Jean d'Or; enjoy the afternoon with the boys," Janette said as I was getting out of the car.

I waited for a few minutes until they left. Oliver was waiting for me inside. He did not come outside to see his parents because he felt too ashamed.

"Are they gone?" Oliver asked.

"Yes, they are. Why do you have to do things you know that you'll regret afterwards?" I asked.

"I don't know . . . I guess I need to be around my friends. That's why I need you to help me change them so I won't feel alone," Oliver said.

"No human can change another human. Only God can change you and your friends. All I can do is to help you guys understand the truth. That's all," I replied.

I greeted everyone while Oliver was introducing me. Oliver's friends also introduced themselves before we started our conversation. Some were excited; others, I could feel, were there just to please Oliver.

"Can you bring another menu? We have one more with us," Oliver informed the waitress, then continued. "I hope you're hungry, because we are going to eat and spend some more time here. I need my friends to hear about God from you. I told them that I have become a Christian and they thought I was going crazy; so, I need you to help me on this," Oliver said to me.

"Thanks Oliver for bringing your friends to hear about the goodness of God. I am sure God will manifest Himself today," I said.

"I sure hope so. We've been together since grade seven. So, It'd be awesome if we can do this Christianity stuff together too."

'Oh boy!' I felt inwardly. If God could change Oliver's friends, then there could be a transformation in Oliver's life too. Then, I prayed silently, 'Oh Lord come into me while I am speaking to these young people. Let your Holy Spirit speak through me and be present in this place.'

The waitress came out with a jug of water and filled my glass while we were waiting for our orders.

"Oliver, why didn't you bring your friends to church today?" I asked, pretending to know nothing about what had happened.

"Sorry, I had to help them do something this morning . . . next time for sure," Oliver replied.

"I see," I said.

I looked Oliver in the eye while he was lying about helping his friends and gave him a knowing look.

"I will let you know what happened later," Oliver said quietly.

"Oh, I know what happened. You snuck out of your room when we were sleeping," I said with a smile.

"I know . . . I couldn't help it man! I wanted to go out. I know that sounds lame," Oliver said. "I promise I won't do it again."

"Oliver . . . don't promise me anything! Promise yourself and your God. All you do—it's between you and your God. Really, *Christians don't judge or hate other people—only sin itself.* There is a saying: 'Don't hate the player, hate the game.'"

Oliver gave me a blank stare, so I continued. "I know it will take a while to understand the goodness of God. However, if you commit yourself, He can transform your life. Always remember this—'*Walk the Talk*,'" I said.

"What do you mean by 'Walk the Talk?'" Oliver asked.

"It means to do what you say you're going to do."

"Ok . . . I am going to. It's just that my friends don't really want to understand," Oliver said.

While I had been talking to Oliver, some were talking to one another; but, others were listening to our conversation and showing some interest.

"Do you guys go to church?" I asked.

"Not really," Oliver's girlfriend Grace answered. "I can't remember the last time I went."

"Do you read the Bible? I am assuming you know what a Bible is?"

"Of course I know! Everyone knows what the Bible is. Come on man, I just don't read it," Grace replied.

"Yeah man . . . we all know what a Bible is," one of the others said in support of Grace.

"Great! In that case, we are on the same page," I continued. "I'm certain that you've heard people on the street or in the mall saying things like 'Jesus or God loves you' haven't you?" I asked.

"Yeah bro," Peter, another friend of Oliver's, replied.

"Do you believe that Jesus or God loves you?"

"I guess so. I can't say that I've ever met him, so how would I know if He loves me," Peter replied rather smugly.

"You are right. You can never meet Him when you are still blind. But do you want to meet Him?" I asked.

"What do you mean? How am I still blind?" Peter asked. He obviously wasn't happy with my strong statement.

"When you don't know something that is true, it's as if you are blind. It's like getting an education. Some people might tell you that it's not important, because they themselves are uneducated and are therefore blind to the importance of it. So it's the same with living an ideal life in Christ."

"Living an ideal life; what do you mean by that? Is that like being rich or something?" Grace asked.

"Not necessarily being rich . . . but being happy. It's a choice of living a completely fulfilled and happy life," I said.

"I think we are pretty happy already; right guys?" Grace commented.

"Listen guys! I think Jean d'Or has the right idea," Oliver intervened.

"I totally understand you if you say that you are happy," I continued. "But sin only gives us temporary happiness which eventually turns into regrets, failures, and sadness. But true happiness can only be found in goodness. And the only way to have that goodness is to have God in our hearts. Because God is good, He brings goodness to us too."

I was on a roll, so I kept talking.

"When we have received the goodness of God in our hearts, we are to do good things and not evil acts. And the only way to reach the goodness of God is to accept Jesus Christ as our Saviour. Jesus is the only way to eternal life. That's what I would call an 'ideal life'. You can have a life which is full of happiness and success. It's not only about having money—it's about possessing everything that is good. God is everything that we need in order to be successful and happy."

As I spoke, I looked directly into their eyes and began to ponder. When we look at these non-believers, these rich people, they look really happy outside; but, inside they are hurting. They look successful with all their fancy cars, beautiful houses, good jobs, and good vacations; but, nothing really satisfies their hearts because they have forgotten that *success is the joy you get out of your achievements.*

When I looked at Oliver's friends I saw a group who appeared outwardly to have it all; but, I knew that, on the inside, they were hurting. They were living self–absorbed lives; they still felt empty because they were missing the goodness of God.

I opened my Bible and taught them about God's goodness. I explained how much love He showed us by sending His only son to die for our sins on the cross. We read three verses. First we read Romans 6:23: 'For the wage of sin is death, but the free gift of God is eternal life in Christ Jesus our Lord.' I went on to say that, because we sinned, someone had to pay the price for that sin. As sinners we were all condemned to hell; but, because Jesus paid that price, we could accept that eternal life in heaven, as the Bible promises.

The second verse that we read was John 3:16. I repeated again how God loves us so much that 'He gave His only son to die for our sins.' And then we read the third verse which was 1John 1:9 which speaks about confessing our sins. We also talked about the Ten Commandments in the Bible and learned about loving God with all our hearts. I suggested Bible readings for all of them on their own time. "Here are some verses which really helped me when I was learning how to trust God and to pray as well," I said. "These verses are: 'Luke 11:1-13; John 14:12-14; 1John 5:14, 15; James 5:13, 16; and Psalms 66:17, 20.'"

That day, three of Oliver's friends, including Peter, were convinced and received Jesus Christ as their Saviour.

At that moment, I made a decision. "Let's read Luke 11:1-13 before you leave to give you some understanding."

"Oh I know that one," Grace said. "My dad used to make us pray that prayer over and over again. Man, I hate it somehow!"

"Is your family Christian?" I asked.

"Yeah . . . her dad is a pastor in France," Oliver said. "Grace came here five years ago as an international student to study theology but she switched over to music to be a rapper."

"You mean she was a Christian before . . . What is she studying again? Music? Christian music?" I asked.

"No, regular music; she is a good rapper. Give him some some, yo," Oliver said to her.

Grace started rapping and she was actually really good.

"You are talented Grace! You know that you can rap for God too," I said.

"I don't think so," she said. "I want to be a star—Christians want things for free. They don't buy records. I want to make cash money . . . Yo . . . you dig what I'm sayin? I used to sing when I was still back home in France and actually did make some Christians albums. But, only a few people supported my records; most of them wanted it for free. They forget that I invested a lot of money and time to get it out there," Grace said.

"But you were a Christian; so . . . what happened to you?" I asked.

"I was born Christian; but, I never had time to explore myself outside of Christianity. So, I decided to drop it for a while to see how others are benefiting from this world," Grace said.

"Are you planning to return to Jesus one day?" I asked.

"Possibly, but not probably," Grace said, shrugging her shoulders.

"Ok. I guess you know better about your life than I do. But have you thought about the consequences of dying outside of God's hands?" I said.

Oliver then spoke up. "Grace . . . I want to change my life and become a true Christian. I am really tired of this life and I also want to be a better son for my parents. They love me and I can't go on this way without any purpose. I am going to follow God . . . so are you with me or not?" Oliver pleaded with Grace.

"Honey . . . there is nothing there. I have done it before, believe me. This is the only life. When I become a star, we will be able to live on our own and forget about our parents' support," Grace replied to Oliver.

"No Grace. I really want to give my life to God. I have never seen my dad as happy as he is now. God has saved my parents' marriage; so, I think He's worth trusting and following," Oliver said with determination.

"I am with you bro. You have my back," Peter said with a determined voice.

Peter was a quiet kid; but, he appeared to be very smart—the kind of person who thinks things through before making decisions. I learned later that his father is a Senator in the government. He was not someone who was there for Oliver's money. He was a university student who often encouraged Oliver to go back to school. The other three were Oliver's followers . . . they went where he went. So, they agreed to become Christians as well.

"So . . . you are telling me that, if I don't come with you, it's over for us?" Grace asked.

"All I am saying is that I want to change my life. I am not happy with it; now that I know the truth about God, I want to serve Him. I want to 'Walk the Talk,'" Oliver replied.

"But you are the one who turned me on to this rap music thing. I was a good girl before you came into my life. Is that how you '**Walk the Talk**?'" Grace spoke sarcastically.

"I am sorry that you let me lead you away from a Christian life; but, you didn't have to let me do it you know. You could have told me about Christianity. Don't blame me. I didn't know anything different at the time. Besides, I still love you. You can still follow God with me," Oliver said.

The argument between Oliver and his girlfriend continued; but, they couldn't agree with one another. Finally, Grace slammed her glass down on the table and walked out of the restaurant.

The waitress came and Oliver paid the bill. Then we shared a prayer with his friends who had just received Jesus Christ as their Saviour for the first time in their lives.

After the prayer, we all exchanged our phone numbers and email addresses and promised to keep in touch. Then, Oliver drove me back to Hamilton.

"Man, I can't believe my girlfriend won't come back to God. Oh well—at least she knows God. I don't know Him very well yet; but, I'm happy for the chance," Oliver commented.

"You may still be able to influence her through your example. And you can pray that God will change her heart," I said. "What is your plan if she does not follow you?"

"I would have no choice but to choose God. I want to prioritize God in my life and be part of my family. Look how happy Mom and Dad are together now. I don't want to stand in their way. I want to be with them," Oliver said sincerely.

"Thank you brother; call me when you get home," I said.

"No! Thank you for coming to help convince my friends about God. I am so happy now that they will come with me to church. Let us know when we can go next."

"I will. Remember to 'Walk the Talk,'" I said as we parted.

I watched him drive away before I entered my apartment. One of my Christian roommates was waiting for me to talk and pray; but, I was too tired for any conversation. So we only prayed together. My final prayer before bed included Grace.

As I relaxed on my couch before heading to bed, I thought about the good things which had happened earlier with Oliver's friends. I concluded that: *'People will always listen, as long as you have something good to say.'*

Self-Development

The next day was Monday—I did not have any classes that day. I slept in and then had a leisurely breakfast. Just as I was finishing my, my roommate came by.

"Good morning Jean d'Or. Did you have a good night?" my roommate Louis asked.

"Yes, I did, thank you. And you?" I replied.

"Yes, thank you. I have a few friends from my class who are struggling with a few problems on how to manage their priorities in life. Some of them are just newborn Christians. They really need help. I told them about you and how much you have helped me with the same struggles. They would like to meet with you. When do you have a free time?" Louis asked.

"I have some time this evening, if they are available," I replied.

"Yes . . . I will call them and I think it should work out well. What time?" Louis asked.

"How about after supper around 7:00 p.m.? That way we can go for coffee at Starbucks on the corner," I said.

"Perfect timing! I will let them know and I am certain that they would be happy to meet," Louis said.

After my breakfast, I called Oliver to see if he and his friends could join us at Starbucks as well. I figured that they were likely to be struggling with some of the same issues and would be able to benefit from the conversation as well.

"Hi Oliver. How's it going? Did you have a good drive back home yesterday evening?" I asked.

"Yes I did. And thank you for being with us yesterday afternoon. My friends and I had a wonderful time chatting with you," Oliver replied.

"Good! I am glad they did because I would like to see if all of you would like to meet again today. My roommate, some of his classmates and I are meeting this evening to talk about self-development and some of the things that we struggle with as young people nowadays. Do you think you and your friends can make it this evening at 7:00 p.m.?" I asked.

"I would love to and will definitely be there; but, I don't know about the others because it's kind of short notice. However, I will bring whoever is available," Oliver assured me.

As old-time Christians, we have to help those newborn believers—to keep in touch, and to follow up with them. Otherwise, it would be a time wasted. I was happy to hear that Oliver was coming. I knew that he and his friends still needed someone to disciple them and that they needed much more than just a one-time meeting. This was part of the reason that I had invited them to join us.

At about five minutes to seven, I received text messages from both Louis and Oliver telling me that they were already at

Starbucks and waiting for me. I responded that I was on the way. When I arrived, I saw that the two groups were sitting in different spots because they didn't know each other yet. I called them both together and we introduced ourselves to one another. I extended my hand to everyone.

"My name is Jean d'Or. Who do we have here?" I asked.

Louis introduced his friends. "Here we have Samantha, George, Desiree, and Belle. Samantha has been a Christian since she was a little girl, but the rest are new Christians."

"And these are my good friends Peter, Lee and his girlfriend Kaylee," Oliver replied.

We decided to choose another spot that had more room and was more comfortable. We settled around a fireplace.

It was Louis who spoke first. "I have known Jean d'Or for about three months. He has been a very good motivator for me. I am so glad that he is my roommate. He is a very nice guy and he's faithful to his God. You can't imagine how much I bother him daily; but, he never complains about it. I am sure you are going to enjoy hearing what he has to say."

"I agree with that," Oliver said. "I know him through my father. Man, I've got to tell you, he's got my attention!"

"Thank you folks for your introduction," I said. "But the accolades belong to God, not to me, because He is the one who works through me. By the way, it's good to have all of you here."

"Thank you. We can't wait to hear what you are going to tell us," Samantha said. "I guess Louis has maybe told you a bit about the things that we are struggling with."

"He touched on some things. I am certain that we are going to have a very good time together this evening and that God's Holy Spirit will lead us," I said.

We all ordered some drinks and began to talk.

"So, folks . . . Louis told me that you are trying to learn about being successful Christians in the marketplace by being able to identify what is good and what is evil. Basically, you are trying to live a spiritual life by doing what's good. Am I right?"

"Kind of . . . ," Samantha answered. "I am sometimes confused about how to balance the Christian life with a successful career. I wonder if I can really get ahead in life and still follow Christ."

"Right. Well, I have prepared a topic to discuss. Self–Development involves our bodies, souls and spirits. Others may call this 'Self–Improvement'. We are going to learn what we should do and how we should do it to develop ourselves."

"Good! I can't wait to hear it," Samantha said with a smile on her face.

"Wow . . . I have lots of expectations placed on me today. That's good! Guys . . . I read every book that can have an impact on me. I would encourage you to start reading books that may influence your lives positively. Also, I would ask you to take notes—but only if you feel like doing it. You know . . . to live a Christian life is the most essential thing to me; I need to make sure that everything I do reflects God's Image. Believe me, it's not easy because you have to devote yourself to it; but it's the best way to live an earthly life. So the basic question we should ask ourselves as Christians—is God okay with the goals that I am pursuing? Some Christians may judge this wrong because they haven't taken enough time to learn the Bible and try to relate their struggles to it."

"What do you mean?" Samantha asked.

"What I mean is straight–forward. When I set a goal, I always ask myself, 'Is God with me on this?' Some Christians may judge it right or wrong . . . but what about God? What does God think about it? Do you think God wants you to fail?" I paused; then, I continued. "Of course, not! He wants us to do better, remain balanced and be happy so that we can serve and praise Him happily. When you think of what I just said—do you think God wants us to stay inactive, or do little?' When you are trying to develop yourself for the better, the devil always tries to get in your way. But all you have to do is to fight and keep faith in God—pray for guidance. So what do you think God wants for us?"

"I think God wants the best for us," Samantha commented.

"I agree! Look at it this way. God Himself put different choices in front of us: succeed, survive or suffer. If you pick succeed, then you must do what it takes to be successful. And if you want just to stay alive, that is your choice too. However, suffering? Huh . . . that's not something we would wish to see happening in our lives. God wants us to be successful in good things we do. The evidence of this is found throughout the Bible. The key is to identify that kind of success we are talking about. If we follow how the Bible defines success, we won't have any doubt or confusion."

"Wow, I see!" Samantha exclaimed.

"I am sure you have read or heard that we are created in the image of God. We are to reflect that image. Yes, God is perfect and, of course, we cannot be perfect. But I know that I have to do my best to reflect His Image by honouring Him in everything I do," I said.

And I know this.

"God gives us power through His Holy Spirit to choose the right path and to change our lives. He gives us wisdom to know the good from the bad. He makes everything we need to reflect His Image available to us. But . . . He has also given us the freedom to make the choice of whether or not we take his free gifts and resources. When we choose the right path or we pray about the plans we are about to pursue, He answers us and sends us His Holy Spirit to lead us. He gives us energy and power to do it; however, the decision is still ours. The Bible says we should be holy as He is holy. This means that our actions should represent that holiness," I explained.

"But the Bible says that no one is perfect. I know that God is holy; but . . . now you are saying that we should be holy. And God is the only one who is holy as far as I know," Louis said.

"True . . . but the holiness that I am talking about is the one that keeps us from doing bad things, taking a wrong path, making bad decisions and wrong plans. So we have to watch what we do and how we do it. But we also have to watch not to become too self-righteous and too full of pride," I emphasized.

"How does righteousness transfer into self-righteousness?" Desiree asked.

"Good question! We have to make sure that God is involved in our self-development. Otherwise, we can stand back and give praise to ourselves. We can end up saying things like: 'Look at me now, look what I have done or see what a great person I have become.' What we should be saying is: 'God is good . . . look how much He has improved my life . . . He has given me the power to change and to develop myself and to give all the glory to Him—He deserves it all!' Above all, we work on our self-development and, at the same time, we display the power of God in our success."

"Thank you, Jean d'Or. I kind of understand now," Desiree said.

"Let's talk about how we are created. Simply . . . we are created in three parts: body, soul and spirit. It is obvious that we tend to own our bodies and do anything we want with them. When I was in Bible College, I learned that our bodies are the physical structure and make–up of a man. In this portion of our being there are certain needs, desires, feelings, and appetites. This physical body is of the earth but blessed by God. Contrary to religious thinking, it is not evil. However, without the control of the Holy Spirit, our needs, desires, and appetites can go beyond the boundaries set by God. Our bodies were created and honoured by God. The Bible says in Romans 12:1-2: 'Therefore I urge you, brethren, by the mercies of God, to present your bodies a living and holy sacrifice, acceptable to God, which is your Spiritual service of worship. And do not be conformed to this world, but be transformed . . . . "Now we can understand how our bodies play a big role in self–development."

"Wow . . . true information! What about our soul?" Desiree asked.

"Our souls refer to the life we are given. Within, we find: our identity, human nature, personality and character. Basically, the soul is the divider between our bodies and spirits. Our souls may express: sorrow, joy, anger, grief and other human emotions through our bodies."

"So what's different between our bodies and our souls?" Peter asked.

"Great question Peter! The difference is that our bodies feel physical things and our souls feel and express emotions. Also, the reasoning of the mind is operated from the soul."

"Mind? How is the mind operated from the soul? Our mind is our brain, not our soul," Belle argued.

"Good thinking, Belle. But our conscious mind lies in the soul and is that part of us which is the front line between spiritual and carnal thought. Our mind is the place where we store information that is received and sent through our spirit. The spirit is the only way to communicate with God. It manifests itself through the soul and body; however, it is transformed by God as the Bible says in Romans 12:2: 'And do not be conformed to this world, but be transformed by the renewing of your mind, so that you may prove what the will of God is, that which is good and acceptable and perfect.' When we renew our minds, we basically increase our wisdom—and there is a big difference between knowledge and wisdom."

"Oh! What's different? It sounds the same to me," Oliver exclaimed.

"Is it being smart?" George added.

"No, they aren't the same. Knowledge is information; but, wisdom is defined as proper understanding and application of knowledge. Many people may have knowledge but only some have wisdom. However this gift is available for any Christian. All we need to do is to ask for it and it will be given to us. Knowledge and wisdom are a part of the will; will is the power we use to apply our knowledge and wisdom. We may have the knowledge of how to do something or the wisdom of how to apply our knowledge; however, we might not have the will to actually do it. An example of this is someone who knows that they should quit smoking. There is a lot of information out there about how to do it . . . lots of wisdom of why it should be done. Yet, thousands of people still die every year with cancer caused by smoking. They can't quit because they don't have the will–power. However, we can make our will strong and be able to accomplish those things which we cannot do easily."

"How can we do that?" Samantha asked.

"Prayer and practice! We can make our will strong through prayer. Ask God to strengthen us inside and outside. Most of the time, we need both of them because they work together somehow. For example . . . a disabled person may be motivated to do things that lead to success but be discouraged because of their physical disability. However, if they have the knowledge and the will, many of them will still reach their goals."

"So you say that practice is the key to strengthening our will?" Samantha asked.

"The Bible says: 'Ask and you shall receive.' When we pray for something, God answers our prayers. But, prayer alone won't do it unless we use those answered prayers to strengthen the gifts we have prayed for. *It doesn't matter how many times we pray, we still have to put our gifts into practice.* Once we start to practice those gifts, it strengthens our will and makes it easier for us to do the things we have dreamed of."

"So . . . how do body, soul and spirit relate to self–development?" Samantha asked.

"They are connected to self–development in different areas. Let's look at these facts. God gave us a body that we should treat properly. We should eat healthily, exercise, and refrain from things that can make us sick. What we do with our bodies also affects our souls and spirits. And what we feed into our souls and spirits will affect our bodies as well. If it's good, then we will manifest good fruit in our lives and the world benefits. But if it's evil, then the world suffers from it."

"But, why is it so hard to develop good character even if I have prayed for it?" Louis questioned.

"Nothing worthwhile comes easy," I said. "And *if you want to succeed, you have to surrender to it. You have to do it. Do it, even if you don't want to!* I have a friend his name is Jude Akom, he inspires me. He works harder than anyone I know. When he landed in Canada, he learned that he was in a different culture, so he had to adjust himself in order to adopt the Canadian way of doing things. He told me: "Do it . . . even in those hard times when you don't feel like it." I have another friend who is retired from teaching. I call him Father. He is already retired but he still volunteers in the community and the way that he contributes makes me want to do more. And we see other young teens around who are changing the world by doing amazing things. The question is: Why not me? Why can't I do the same?"

I continued. "Yes Louis, we pray. But, God is not going to do your job for you. He will send a helper for certain and strengthen your will; but, you need to train your will to make it work. Also, God wants us to be strong and mature so that we don't get deceived into thinking that our success came from our own effort. I can tell you that *the value of something comes from the pain of getting it.* Jesus did! He took the pain on the cross to complete his mission for saving us. The most important thing is to use the opportunities God has blessed us with to bless others who are still struggling."

"I would like to speak to you about myself as an illustration. When I landed here in Canada, I could have decided to stay on social assistance. But, I decided to go back to college, although I already had a degree back home. When I graduated from theological studies and didn't get a job in the field I graduated from, I could have just sat at home and collected social assistance. Instead, I woke up my will—power and decided to do something different. Today, thanks to God, I am back in college to develop myself and my skills and increase my qualifications. Yes, it is hard; but, when we ask God to strengthen our will—and we put it into practice—it becomes strong and is able to accomplish those tough things."

I paused for a breath; then, I continued speaking from my heart. "Here are a few things that may hinder our self—development. Some people are just plain lazy and want others to take over their responsibilities. Another reason might be that we feel we are victims of our failures. Instead of getting up and going forward, we sit down and blame ourselves. If we don't blame ourselves, then we might blame others. But for self—development to happen, we must stop blaming and push hard to develop our will until we get it right."

"That is true," Peter, Oliver's friend, said. "Just out of curiosity, where do you get all this knowledge and wisdom of yours? Everything you are telling us sounds so real."

"Yeah . . . I'm wondering the same thing. How do you do that?" Louis asked too.

Peter was a very smart young man who was attending law school. Sometimes it can be a challenge to convince highly intelligent people because they believe so strongly in their own knowledge. Peter wasn't one to argue; but, he didn't easily agree either. I knew that Peter had great potential and would be able to help his friend Oliver and the others once he had these issues worked out for himself.

"Thanks Peter. I get this kind of knowledge and wisdom from different sources. Most important for me is to pray constantly, asking for wisdom—as the Bible recommends." I continued. "There are two powerful words that I live by when I am in process of pursuing something—constantly and until. Pray, ask, do it, study, read, educate yourself *constantly until* you get it. So we need to pray constantly until we receive it."

"Along with prayer, I read books, attend seminars, and listen to experts' advice and experiences to increase my knowledge. Then I apply it in my life to make it work. I also have a high regard for education. I make sure that I pay attention in all my courses, follow what my teachers teach me to do and use my time efficiently. Finally, I apply wisdom and knowledge together," I added.

"How do you apply knowledge and wisdom?" Peter asked again.

"Good question Peter. When I have obtained knowledge of something that I need to present, then I pray for the wisdom to present it so that it will be clearer or have more effect. Basically, wisdom is an addition to the knowledge—it's a gift from God to boost our knowledge if we have prayed for it. Getting knowledge isn't enough by itself; we have to apply wisdom to it. Above all, we have to do this effectively and efficiently so that it does not produce such fatigue while doing it that it may cause us to quit."

"What do you mean to do it effectively and efficiently?" Oliver asked.

"Let me describe it in a way that relates to what we are talking about here today. What I am talking about is choosing a right path that will allow us to develop ourselves in a way that will not cost us a lot of time and energy."

"And how do you do that?" Samantha asked.

"Just pray and believe it. Ask God to do the big part of your plan and you do the small part. Here is my secret for how I accomplish tough things. I always pray about everything. However, there are those things you don't just pray for but supplicate. Every time I am doing this, I'm speaking to myself the phrase: 'I know I can do it in Jesus' name.' I use that name over and over until I get it. That's my secret. Use Jesus' name in those things you struggle with. It's called 'supplication.'"

"Wow! God has really blessed us this evening! I am glad that I came. I was very tired and I considered not coming; but, this lesson is kind of refreshing to me," George said.

It was getting late and some of us had classes in the morning. Others, such as Oliver and his friends, had to drive a long distance.

"I hope this lesson has been helpful to you," I said. "Here are four steps I want to wrap up with regarding self–development:

1. Pray: Pray for wisdom and strength of your will,
2. Plan: Choose a right path to work on to self-develop; this could be education or something else,
3. Practice: Put your plan into practice,
4. Combine wisdom, will, and knowledge and see what happens.

Trust me; if you do apply these four steps correctly, self-development will happen!"

Everyone was very happy to learn how God's will works within our self–development. I was already noticing that Oliver's behaviour had improved since he accepted Jesus Christ as his saviour. He was now polite, laid–back and a good listener. Praise God for the change in Oliver!

"Thanks Jean d'Or. We have learned a very important lesson that will help us in our struggles. I would like to hear more of your wisdom. Can I ask you to come speak to our youth group? We get together twice a month; most of the time we have about two hundred youth. Can you please come?" Samantha asked.

"I think I can do that if I know ahead of time so I can plan for it," I replied.

"Thanks. I will inform you ahead of time," Samantha said.

"Actually, I was thinking of asking if we can have our own regular meetings—maybe once a month or every week. But, I guess you are too busy for weekly meetings," Belle said in a polite manner.

"Weekly meetings are a bit much for me; but, I don't mind monthly meetings. Please, let me know whenever you need to talk. We can make time as long as it does not fall on the weekend because I have another meeting I usually attend," I replied.

"Great! Thanks again," Belle said.

We all prayed together before we left.

"See you on Saturday at the meeting, Oliver." I told him this discreetly because the meeting on Saturday wasn't for everyone—only those who were invited.

"Right Jean d'Or. I will talk to you later," Oliver said as he and Peter left together.

As we were leaving, I said to Louis, Samantha, George and Belle: *'Keep moving forward, increase your capabilities in prayer, focus on your business more than you focus on others' business, search for God's wisdom, spend more time on self–development, and believe in yourselves.'*

God's Economy

It was a beautiful Saturday! Thomas had called Frank and Mark earlier with the news that he was moving back to England to take care of some of his family business. He asked Frank if it would be okay to have his lesson that week as he did not know if he would ever be part of the group again. Mark requested that, if we were going to meet earlier than usual, we do so at his church due to another meeting he had to attend following our meeting. James and his family had never been to Mark's church; so, I was glad that we were having it there.

We all arrived on time that day; Pastor Mark was waiting for us to open the church door himself.

"Hello everyone. Welcome! I wasn't sure that all of you got my message."

"Wow, I like the decor of this church. God's resources have been wonderfully used," Janette commented with a smile on her face.

"That's true. Where God is, His blessings flow like a river. Yes, we are blessed . . . I thank God that we can use His resources to bless others," Mark replied.

He closed the church door behind us and we took an elevator to go to his office where the meeting would be held. We got to his office and were surprised at what we saw. All of us, except for James and Janette, had attended some church services here; but, this was the first time that some of us had been in Mark's office. It was one of the biggest and best–equipped offices that I had ever seen! It was divided by furniture that produced different areas. There was a section where he spent time studying, another for meetings—it was set up like a living room with immaculate furniture—and there was even a section to host a meal! Additionally, behind bookshelves, there was a little door that led to a small prayer room.

Pastor Mark spoke openly. "Please do not get the wrong idea from my office. We have a lot of wealthy, educated professionals come through here; often these people look on the outside first before they will listen to you. They want to see how God has blessed you on the outside before they look on the inside. Most of them are afraid to come to Jesus because they feel their lives will be worse and they will have to give up everything they own. They don't understand that God wants our hearts and souls—not our money. We have another office that we regularly use downstairs. Today though, you are Ambassadors of God and you deserve to be seated here in what I call "God's Blessing Office." Please sit back and relax. Let's hear about the goodness of God from Thomas' lesson for today."

I thought for a moment about what Mark had just said. It sounded true. God gives us all the resources to be used for His glory.

"I am very impressed; can you please give us a tour of your church before we start our meeting?" James asked.

"Of course I can. I was going to do it later; but, let's do it now. We may not have enough time after," Pastor Mark replied.

As Mark began our tour, we followed with anticipation. "The church is about 20 years old. This place used to be a plaza and I bought it after I sold my business. After I graduated from theology school in the USA, I decided to honour God. The whole plaza was torn down and we built this beautiful church. Please, follow me down to the sanctuary."

We entered the sanctuary. It was huge and beautiful. It was divided down the middle and on two sides and had two levels—the main part and the balcony. It felt very relaxing. It was the kind of place where you just wanted to stay and worship God. Although I had been there before, I had never paid much attention to it. Now it was like I was seeing it for the first time. The folding seats were leather and very comfortable. The platform at the front was formidable and could easily have been mistaken for a high-class concert hall. Nothing I have seen in other churches really compared to it. As we toured the building, I noticed that James really admired everything about the place—but he didn't say anything at that time.

"This is where we praise God every Sunday," Mark said.

"Wow, it's so grand and beautiful! There is no way that God wouldn't hear your praise from this place," Janette said smiling.

"Thank you, Janette. Again it is a way to thank Him and give Him glory for his love towards us. And I want everyone who comes here to His house to feel welcomed," Mark replied.

"I wish everyone in the whole world could do the same or think the same way as you," Thomas said.

"I am sure there are lots of people who feel the same or do the same. We are just not enough yet; but, we will get there one day. That's why we are here to present good examples as we represent God's image on earth," Mark added.

He showed us every corner of the church, including the small office he had told us about, the big library and another place downstairs that looked like a restaurant.

"Do you have a restaurant here?" Janette asked.

"No. It's a place where we offer snacks and refreshments after the Sunday service as well as during or after any special events or services that we might have during the week. We also host meals for homeless people three times a week," Mark said.

"Good for you! No wonder you are so blessed," Janette complimented.

We admired the place he was talking about which hosts the homeless—it was incredible to see! It was more beautiful than some high–class restaurants!

"Please let me take you up to the roof. There is something I want to show you there," Mark said.

We took the elevator to get there; as we walked out of the elevator and onto the roof, we were surprised to see a large helicopter which looked brand new.

"Whoa, look at that!" I said as I stared at the helicopter.

"We just bought it a month ago. We use it to deliver aid—including food, clothing, and medication—to those reserve lands where cars can't reach," Mark informed us.

"Beautiful! I have heard about churches which did this kind of thing; but, I have never seen it for myself. Thank God that I came to know Jean d'Or or I would have never seen this," James spoke in awe. "You said reserve lands; what do you do there?" He asked with interest.

"We decided to add this mission to what we do here. We deliver God's good news to reserve lands because those people need to hear the goodness of God. And we don't just tell them about God; we also demonstrate His love by providing them with food, clothes, medication and other essentials. In our church, we have a few doctors and nurses who volunteer to go there and treat those people for free," Mark said. "Oh, I forgot to take you to the basement. Let's go there and I can show you the types of things we usually provide."

We went to the basement and found it to be full of supplies such as canned food, clothing, first aid kits and vitamins.

"My wife and I have been thinking about some volunteer work that we can get involved in," James said. "We were thinking of doing something with a refugee program. Your commitment to God has really touched my heart. I love what you do for God's glory and I would personally like to get involved in your ministry and missions. I believe my wife would love to join me too," James said.

"Yes, I would love to as well," Janette confirmed.

"Thanks James and Janette. I am sure that God is pleased," Mark complimented.

"Pastor Mark . . . I have a question for you. Why have we never seen you or your church on T.V or heard you on the radio? Since I started to learn about God, my wife and I sometimes watch a few preachers on T.V., such as Joel Osteen. Why aren't you televised?" James asked.

"Good question. When I was studying theology, I learned that a good way to convince people is to be with them. I like Jean d'Or's expression: 'If you want to catch fish, don't fish in the boat, but in the sea where there are many fish uncaught yet'. Everyone who has access to TVs and radios has already heard the good news of God. But there are many around the world who cannot get the access to technology. So, while I think TVs or radios are effective, news is better when you do public appearances. God also wants His good news to reach those who are more unreachable. Those fish are still in the sea—not the ones in the boat already. And that is who we target," Mark responded.

"I love your mission; it is so clear. D'Or, why did you never mention this church to us? Why did you take us to a different one?" James said.

"I wanted you to visit many churches and learn the difference so you could decide for yourselves which one you like better. However, I was going to bring you here too," I replied.

"Well, I guess this is it. Right, Janette? We are going to join this church starting today," James said.

"Thank you Lord! You are very welcome here!" Pastor Mark exclaimed. Let's go back to the office for our meeting. We have taken so much time touring the church. Let's take no more time out of Thomas' lesson."

So, we went back to the big office to start our meeting. Frank as usual opened with prayer and the introduction of our speaker for that day.

"As I informed you earlier, Thomas is leaving us. But I will let him tell us the details. I believe it will be his last lesson with us," Frank said.

Mark left the office for a few minutes and returned with a few bottles of soft drinks for our refreshment.

"I know we are not going to have time after the lesson; so, let's make a toast to Thomas." We bowed prayerfully. "May God be with you and protect you always, Thomas." We responded with a unified 'Amen.'

"Thank you all. You are my true friends. I am going far away; but, I will be always close to you in my heart. Please . . . always include me in your prayers," Thomas said with feeling.

Thomas also prayed and thanked God before he started his lesson.

"In my lesson for today, we are going to talk about 'God's Economy'. I will abbreviate my remarks because I don't want you to get bored with my lesson," Thomas laughed.

"Great! I can't wait to hear the solutions that God inspired you with regarding this failing economy," Valerie said with a grin.

"Great Val! But, it's not something that you haven't heard before. In fact, maybe you've heard it a million times. It is part of my economics course that I teach at the college. The difference is that, at the college, we don't include God in the course."

"That's all right, Thomas. We're not in school today," Valerie joked in her usual friendly manner.

Thomas began. "Nowadays, we tend to depend only on ourselves. Since I became a believer in God and started teaching business courses including economics in college, I discovered that people who possess a lot of money can affect the economy by the way their money is used."

"What do you mean by that?" James asked.

"What I mean is simple. One person may possess too much money and have it inactive. On the other hand, he or she may have millions or billions of dollars in the bank. The money is just sitting there and isn't working to boost the economy. So, who gets benefit from those millions? Only two people: the bank owners and the investors. You may even find that the employees don't get raises or the bank owners don't hire more employees because those millions of dollars are invested for their purpose. And who suffers? Poor people who have little. The money should be used for creating more activities to benefit everyone."

Thomas continued. "There is so much money that isn't being circulated throughout the country. People are not able to benefit from it and the economy slows because there is fear in people's hearts. The question is—who is happy? Obviously, only a few people can have everything. This creates fear. And when this kind of fear enters people's lives, it creates dependency on something else other than the truth."

"What kind of dependency does it create?" Valerie asked.

"I'll tell you. People who possess a lot of money start to depend on it too much. Their money comes first in their lives and they don't think about God unless they are believers. So they start to protect it more than they protect the world. They are even afraid to use their wealth to create more business because Satan has put fear in their hearts that they may lose their money if they do so. This kind of fear is from the devil. It creates a dependency and takes away the truth of knowing God and trusting in Him alone. Fear of losing wealth creates the love of it and it blinds people to the fact that money is meant to be used, to get things done on earth, and to bring glory to God by using it in the right way."

"I get it," Janette said.

"The Bible refers to money as an opportunity that God gives us to get his missions work done on earth. So I believe that—if we can think about why some of us have a lot more money than others and why some of us are way more blessed than others—we will find that it isn't because we worked so hard but because God has trusted in us, as good stewards, to use His resources to keep His economy moving. God created this earth, so He loves it; and . . . He gave us all the tools we need to do well and keep His economy balanced. But how do we do it? It depends on the plans we make."

"That's true" Mark agreed.

"I would recommend that we start to make realistic plans. They should be in line with God's plans. If they seem not to be materializing, then maybe they aren't realistic. Who holds the future? Only God holds the future; so, we should make plans according to God's direction. We should know that God is the master of our economy; we need to make our plans serve us to achieve His mission."

"I am convinced! What else?" Frank requested.

"We should not rely too much on our own abilities; rather, we should expect God to work when we set financial goals. This kind of expectation increases our faith and dependency on God. And it also creates a good stewardship for how we spend God's resources. Once we make plans that result in more opportunities for everyone, I believe we will no longer be in this economic crisis."

Thomas paused to take a drink of water before moving forward. "So we should now evaluate our plans and language, then compare them with what is actually happening today. Are our goals being met? Why or why not? Another question is whether the plan is realistic or unrealistic. Was God's original plan included in our actual plans? What about talking the same language; do we still understand each other? Or has our language become confusing due to the fact that we try to do everything under our own power? Those are the questions we should ask ourselves, either as believers or non–believers. If we create a plan based on wrong assumptions, the result will be different from our expectations."

"So what do you suggest we do in our evaluation?" Frank asked.

"Good question Frank. We should:

(a) *Pray for our financial plans* and allow God to control them,
(b) learn how to *split His resources* among us and support those creative–minded individuals,
(c) *Proportionally contribute* to God's plans to boost this economy,

(d) learn how to *share God's tasks* on earth, create and increase more opportunities so everyone with different talents can benefit,

(e) Lastly . . . learn how to take the importance of *opportunity cost*. In economics studies, *opportunity cost* may be defined as 'the value of the best alternative that must be given up for another choice' by Canadian's Economics Editions. By using this term, we learn how we should give up the dependency on money to God's dependency and discover how God wants us to use His resources. Choose God as the number one alternative . . . not just another alternative."

Thomas drew our meeting to an end with a personal thought. "Now it's time, I feel, to be His servant. My call is to help others by serving my Lord. I don't want to serve people for power on earth; I want to serve my God and help others for His glory. I feel that, by doing this, I will overcome the evil temptation of money dependency and gain more dependency on God. So, I will encourage all rich people to come out with a good plan that can boost this economy without having fear, because God is watching. He will not let us down!"

"What a good message!" Janette complimented.

"Thank you guys for coming to listen to me; I will miss you all so much. As I promised, I will keep each of you informed and come often to visit," Thomas concluded.

"Thank you for the lesson. It was a wonderful message and I learned so much from it. Where did you say you are going again?" James asked.

"I am going to England. My grandparents live there and I am going to take care of them. I want to be there for them and not make the same mistake I made towards my parents."

"Then, what are you going to do with your possessions here?" I asked.

"My sisters and some other relatives will come and take care of them. For the time that I am in England, I have set goals I want to accomplish for the Lord. I want to inspire young people; so, we will go around the world to do missionary work and create more opportunities for poor people. I want to fund a program that does this."

"Way to go, Thomas!" I said.

"I am going to join Mark in his mission work plans," James added.

"Good for you, James; God will bless you," Frank said.

"By the way . . . I have a proposal to ask all of you. Can we celebrate with a nice send—off for Thomas tomorrow after the church service?" Mark requested.

"Sounds wonderful!" Valerie exclaimed.

Everyone agreed to be there the next day for Thomas' celebration.

"Let me give you a special parking pass code for tomorrow," Mark said to James. "When you reach the parking lot, go to the left,—there will be a small gate—enter the code and the gate will let you in. That's where special guests and pastors park. One of our ushers will escort you inside the church to where your seats will be."

"Thank you, Mark. See you tomorrow. God bless!" Janette said.

"Jean d'Or . . . could you please come with us to Toronto? We are heading to our nephew's birthday party. That is the reason why Oliver didn't come with us today for the meeting because he has been helping out there," Janette said.

"Yes, I'd like that," I replied.

I left my car at the church underground parking lot. I was going to come back the next day anyway.

"One of your nephews is celebrating a birthday? Do I know him?" I asked.

"We don't think so. But, you will know him soon. And he has heard of you already. We told every family member about Jean d'Or. So they all want to meet you," Janette said.

I was just wearing some casual weekend clothing. I had been wondering why James and Janette were so dressed up; now, I realized it was because they were going to a party.

"Can we go by my home so that I can change to something more presentable?" I requested.

"Ok; but you look fine," Janette commented.

So, we went by my apartment and I changed into some more appropriate clothes. I also felt that I might be spending a night over at their house, so I picked up a few things I might need.

When we got to the party, there were lots of people there of all ages. Many of them, including Oliver, came to the door to welcome us.

"This is Jean d'Or who we have talked about," James expounded.

Everyone was happy to meet me, because they had all noticed the change that God had begun to perform in James.

"Thank you for helping James and his family get back together. The family was in trouble. Look at them now . . . how happy they are," one lady commented.

"Thank you. But, we should thank God for all of this. I'm doing God's mission," I replied.

"No it's you. God did not come from heaven to do what you are doing. Why do some people always say God, God, God—please . . . leave that God alone. He is in heaven. Do you really think he cares about everything that's going on here on earth?" she argued.

I decided not to argue with her point of view, but to let James or Janette work on her since they were family.

I noticed that Oliver wasn't happy at all. "What's going on? I heard you were too busy today," I said.

"A whole lot man . . . a whole lot is going on. My girlfriend, I mean my ex-girlfriend . . . We were taking a break because she did not like the fact that I became a Christian. So, she got mad at me and decided to go back to France—but, she didn't make it. I feel like it's my fault that she died," Oliver spoke with a heavy heart.

"Whoa, wait a minute! What do you mean?" I asked.

"She died in a car accident."

While he was speaking, tears ran down his cheeks. It was a terrible moment for both of us.

'Oh, Heavenly Father! Why couldn't you have just given me another chance to talk to her?' I prayed in my mind.

I felt so sad to hear the news as I listened to Oliver expressing himself with such emotion. I couldn't find any word to say that would comfort him.

Then my heart reached out. "You know Oliver . . . God creates everything; he gives a life and he takes it away. You have decided to believe, trust and follow Him; Grace made a decision to step away from Him. So, it's not your fault that she is gone. It's nobody's fault. Each of us has a different destiny one day. But, the good news is that we can predict our future—because it is in the hands of God.

Oliver . . . we don't really live here on Earth eternally . . . we are just passing through. So it's not your fault."

"But, Jean d'Or—how will God judge her? Is she going to heaven?"

"All I can say to you now, Oliver, is that we can pray for her soul and ask Him to have mercy on her. Let's pray together."

After the prayer, I encouraged Oliver to support his cousin's moment.

"Thanks Jean d'Or; you are really a good friend," he said.

"You have become a good friend to me too, Oliver."

The party went very well and everyone seemed to enjoy themselves. We left a little late. Oliver's parents felt grief for the death of Grace. But, they kept their thoughts private.

We arrived home. Then, I went straight to bed after prayer. 'I wish I could have had another moment to speak to Grace about God's mercy,' I thought.

As I was falling asleep, my final thought was that we need to *always keep our hearts pure enough and ready for the Lord; any moment can be a moment of glory if we are ready for it.*

Choosing an Ideal Life

The next day was Sunday and we woke up early to get ready for church. James and Janette were very excited that they had finally chosen the church which they wanted to join. Oliver was still tired from the party and feeling grief over his ex-girlfriend's death. But, he was willing to join us for church.

"Are you ready?" James shouted with excitement. "Let's go . . . I don't want to be late!"

We got there before the service started. The usher was waiting for us and led us to some seats at the front which were reserved for us. All our group members were there, including Frank and Thomas. This church was full of rich and powerful people with whom I personally would not normally socialize; but, before God, we were together as one family.

Five minutes later, the service started; Pastor Mark welcomed the visitors and announced that there were special guests in the church. Of course, he was talking about James and his family. He asked them to stand and greet the church.

"Hello everyone; I am privileged to be here in the house of the Lord," James said with a smile.

The worship team was incredible and used several different types of instruments. They were all very well-trained; some even used to sing professionally.

"This sounds so real," Oliver said. "I didn't know that it would sound so alive!" He pronounced with excitement. "I wish Grace could have had a chance to see this," he added with sadness in his voice.

"I know Son. You should be up there to do your rap thing for God too," James said with a proud smile.

"One day Dad . . . one day," Oliver replied.

Pastor Mark preached about baptism which appeared to touch Janette's heart. After the service, a lot of people came over to greet and hug James and his family. It was a special moment! The church members made a huge impact on them with their welcome.

"I like this church; people notice that you exist. The last one you took us to, no one came by to even greet us afterwards. It seemed as if no one was interested in knowing about us," James said.

"I am sorry that happened; but not all churches are like that. Many, like this church, are more open to others in terms of approaching visitors," I said.

I noticed that James loved attention. It seemed as if he always wanted people to notice and listen to what he had to say. He was used to getting praise from family, employees, and friends. I personally do not care if people notice my presence. All that matters to me is to give glory to God. I could see that James was still holding on to old, ingrained attitudes.

After the wonderful service, Pastor Mark greeted us.

"Welcome again. I assume you are going to stay for Thomas' celebration."

"Of course we are. Hello, Thomas, how are you?" James asked.

"Good! Did you enjoy the service?"

"Very much—thank you for asking. We hope that it will become our regular church," Janette said.

"Yes, it is a strong church. Mark is a wonderful pastor. He helped me to become who I am today. I became a good Christian because of his dedication to me. He took the time to make certain that I understood what I was learning. I will never forget the day that I received Jesus as my Saviour," Thomas said.

We waited for Pastor Mark to finish up with his responsibilities at the church before we went out for Thomas' celebration.

"Where are you taking me?" Thomas asked.

"Let's go to one of the restaurants by the lakeshore. I know a nice place that has good service. The owner and most of her employees are active members of our church; so, we treat one another as family," Mark said.

One of the waiters greeted us when we arrived at the restaurant. "Hello Pastor . . . the service was wonderful today. I was thinking about getting baptized."

"Thank you for your remarks. I remember my baptism. It was twenty-nine years ago. It was something beautiful that I couldn't compare to anything. Please talk to one of our deacons at the church and they will provide you with information . . . Do you have a table available for all of us? There are ten in our group."

"Of course; your table is always available and reserved. Our boss, Marie, said that, any time you come here, we should have a quiet and comfortable place reserved just for you. She actually suggested that we should always give you her place. Please follow me. I know that you may be a little bit cold. I have some seats available near the fireplace and there is a nice view of the lake from there as well," the waiter spoke quietly to us.

We were seated by the fireplace which was very comfortable. The food we ordered was served right away; so, we gave thanks for the meal.

"This is a nice place; it is very relaxing," James said.

Pastor Mark spoke in agreement. "Yes it is; my wife and I come here often. Actually, we started to come right after its opening. Marie, the owner, wasn't a Christian back then; she is now—a very strong believer. She is involved with many activities in our church."

"Wonderful! Yes, people can change due to our commitment and dedication," Frank added.

After the meal, Marie had ordered cake for Thomas' celebration. As we enjoyed our meal and fellowship time together, Thomas expressed how thankful he was for everything and for the blessings we had placed in his life since we met.

"I thank everyone here for your dedication to me and for the love and caring that you have shown towards me. May God bless and protect all of you." Thomas showed emotion in his eyes while he was speaking.

"Let's pray for his protection; everyone . . . please extend your hand over him," Pastor Mark said.

We prayed that God would bless and protect our friend Thomas.

"Thank you all again," Thomas said. "Jean d'Or, remember to send me a copy of your book once it's done."

"Yes . . . but you will have to visit us to get it," I said smiling.

"What do you mean? We want to read it by next year," Thomas said.

"Well I wasn't really intending to write it just yet. I didn't even think I would do it, since it wasn't part of my goals," I said.

"Plans have a way of changing. When I studied business, I didn't know that I was going to be a teacher of business programs," Thomas said. "I thought that I was just going to keep running my family's business. Jean d'Or, you can do it. Please let me know what you need, so we make certain you get all the support you need. You are a very smart young man and I believe you can accomplish anything you put your mind to. Keep it up."

"Thanks Thomas. I will pray about it and I am sure that God will respond to me. If that's what God wants me to do, He will put it in my heart, strengthen my will and reveal to me how to do it," I said.

We said our goodbyes to one another and left the restaurant. I could feel the emotional bond between us as we watched Thomas leaving the group. We went straight to our cars and left, keeping our feelings to ourselves.

In the months ahead . . .

Our group continued with our weekly meetings. The following spring, James, Janette and Oliver decided to be baptized in water. Pastor Mark, Frank and the rest of our group gave a huge party at James' and Janette's house; everyone in the group as well as James' extended family and friends from Italy were invited. Oliver's friend Peter was also baptized that day. It was an amazing time!

James stood up to speak in front of everyone at the party. "I want to thank you all of your efforts to make this day happen. Above all, I want to thank God for saving my life and my family.

Believe me . . . I was living in hell. I was chasing after money and thoughts of it consumed me. My family was left behind. My wife and I went through lots of counselling . . . but it never did any good. We spent thousands of dollars for nothing. But look at us now! We paid nothing to God for our happiness," James paused; then, he continued to speak from heart. "So I would like to close by advising everyone like me who is going through tough times to consider allowing God to lead your lives. Money will never be enough. It actually creates problems as you get lots of it. It has been said: *'The more you get the more you want.' Getting more money isn't a bad thing; but the whole issue is how you use it.*"

As I listened to James' speech, I could only feel thankfulness to God for the way He had worked in the lives of his family. They had truly been transformed through the grace of God!

It was an unusual celebration. Everyone was extremely happy and wanted to know the rest of our group who helped James and his family to overcome their struggles and restore their marriage. Many of his family weren't Christians . . . but, guess what happened? They responded when Pastor Mark made the invitation to the congregation to step forward for Jesus' salvation! The next Sunday, Pastor Mark's church was full of James' family—it filled nearly half of the church! All the guests' and visitors' seats were taken. Regular pastors and deacons had to sit in regular members' seats. I looked around and marvelled at this miracle which had been performed by God. Something triggered in my mind; some families in this world are more supportive compared to others. If you get one, you get all . . . I found this in James' family. *'This is how families should do it . . . support each other.'*

Two years later . . .

It was nearing time for my graduation. James and his family's lives had been completely changed. Oliver had gone back to school to study music and became the leader of the music committee at church. He was an amazing singer!

Janette started a ladies' Bible study at her house. James and Janette had decided to go to theological school—the same school I attended. I could see that their relationship had truly been solidified by God's hand!

One day . . .

I received a surprise from Janette and James. Before they presented a gift to me, Janette came up to me alone and expressed her thoughts. "Thank you, Jean d'Or, for being there for us—you have been truly an inspiration and I'm certain that God is going to bless you even more than He already has!"

Then, James announced. "D'Or. Janette and I have been thinking of you and would like to thank you for introducing us to God. It has changed our lives completely for the good,"

"And . . . I would like to thank you. You have changed my life too in different ways," I responded.

"Great! We would like to offer you this," James said.

"A key? That's a car key," I said, a little stunned.

James spoke with emotion. "Yes, it's my old Lexus. We noticed that you were having problems with your current car and we decided to give this to you. I love this car! It was my father's . . . He gave it to me when I decided to join him in his business. It was a good gift for a father to give to his son. So, you deserve her—take care of her."

"Thank you so much for the gift. You shouldn't do this though. What about your son? What will he think if he learns that you gave the car to me?"

"Oliver knows and he agrees with our decision. We have done everything necessary for the car to be on the road. All you need to do is to transfer the vehicle to your name and we will pay for that. Let's go to the garage so that I can show you the car," James said.

We went to check out the Lexus. It was a perfect gift!

'Thank you, Jesus, for your love. May your name be glorified!' I prayed silently.

"Come on; let's cruise a little bit in the city so you can get the feel of her," James said.

"I am coming too," Janette said.

I got behind the wheel. After several kilometres, James looked at me. "How is it? I hope you like her," James said.

"I like her. Thank you!" I said.

The vehicle drove very smoothly compared to my old car. The next day, I transferred the vehicle to my name and called all the group members to tell them the good news. Every day I drove the car . . . I thought of how God's generosity can work through people.

Two years after that . . .

Oliver graduated from college where he studied music and production. He decided to stay with his grandpa and grandma in Italy where he started his own music recording company. He sent me a copy of his first Christian record and told me how happy he was to be living his dream and giving praise to God.

In December of that year . . .

Frank decided to leave the group and retired in Germany to be with the rest of his family. He still visits once in a while and is still involved in some activities by donating money to Pastor Mark's church missions.

After Frank left the country . . .

Mark took over the group meetings and held them at his office. James and the others still gather together regularly. As for me, I graduated and decided to move back to my home–town in the Niagara area. But, I still go once in a while to the meetings. They're not the same as they used to be. Each of us has a different life to pursue . . . but, we are all doing God's will. When needed support is necessary though, we are there for each other. I learned so much from this special group! I witnessed that money can be used wisely to serve and honour God. Frank, Thomas, Pastor Mark and the others were being excellent stewards for God. Now, they are living an ideal life!

Today . . .

I can only thank God for how He has worked in my life. I truly feel wealthy in Him! Despite the constant hatred and troubles I experienced in my younger years, God protected me all the way . . .

What lies ahead for me? God knows!

Other Products of this Author:

Gassilde—Troubles of an African Girl

Softcover
978-1-46204-454-2
$11.95

E-Book
978-1-46204-455-9
$.9.99

Hardcover
978-1-46204-456-6
$21.95

*These Author's products may be ordered through booksellers
worldwide or by contacting:*
iUniverse
1663 Liberty Drive
Bloomington, IN 47403
www.iuniverse.com
1-800-Authors (1-800-288-4677)